THE SERMON ON THE MOUNT
Authentic Human Values

THE SERMON ON THE MOUNT

Authentic Human Values

Oscar Stephen Brooks

**UNIVERSITY
PRESS OF
AMERICA**

LANHAM • NEW YORK • LONDON

Copyright © 1985 by

University Press of America,® Inc.

4720 Boston Way
Lanham, MD 20706

3 Henrietta Street
London WC2E 8LU England

Printed in the United States of America

Library of Congress Cataloging in Publication Data

Brooks, Oscar Stephen.
 The Sermon on the mount.

 Bibliography: p.
 1. Sermon and the mount. I. Sermon on the mount.
English 1985. II. Title.
BT380.2.B76   1985   226'.906   85-9120
ISBN 0-8191-4740-0 (alk. paper)
ISBN 0-8191-4741-9 (pbk. : alk. paper)

All University Press of America books are produced on acid-free
paper which exceeds the minimum standards set by the National
Historical Publications and Records Commission.

for

Sally

and Steve, and Philip, and Amanda

Acknowledgement:

> Quotations from the Bible are taken from the
> Revised Standard Version of the Bible
> copyrighted 1946, 1952, 1971, 1973, by the
> Division of Christian Education of the
> National Council of the Churches of Christ in
> the United States of America. Permission to
> use has been granted.

Abbreviations:

> Abbreviation for the books of the Bible are
> those commonly used in scholarly works.
> TDNT = Theological Dictionary of the New
> Testament. Edited by Gerhard
> Kittel. Translated and edited by
> Geoffrey W. Bromiley. Grand Rapids:
> Wm. B. Eerdmans Publishing Company,
> 1964. 10 Vols.

TABLE OF CONTENTS

Acknowledgements................................... iv

Abbreviations iv

Preface viii

  I.   The Sermon................................... 1

 II.   Reading the Sermon........................ 10

            The Design of the Gospel............... 10

            The Beginning Context.................. 13

            The Following Context.................. 16

III.   Ideal Disciples........................... 19

            The Beatitude: The Ideal Person
                Matthew 5:3-10................ 19

            Salt and Light: Jesus' Disciples
                Matthew 5:11-16.............. 29

            The Reader: One of the Disciples....... 31

 IV.   Ethical Values............................ 33

            The Teacher: His Authority
                Matthew 5:17-20.............. 33

            The Instruction: Ethical Values........ 35

                The Value of Human Existence
                    Matthew 5:21-26.............. 38

                The Value of Sexuality
                    Matthew 5:27-32.............. 40

                The Value of Integrity
                    Matthew 5:33-37.............. 46

                The Value of Self Respect
                    Matthew 5:38-42.............. 48

The Value of Love
        Matthew 5:43-48.............. 51

    The Reader: The Instructed............ 56

V. Motivational Values...................... 60

    The Instruction
        Matthew 6:1-18.............. 60

        Almsgiving
            Matthew 6:2-4.............. 61

        Prayer
            Matthew 6:5-15.............. 64

        Fasting
            Matthew 6:16-18.............. 70

    The Reader: The Instructed............ 72

VI. The Ultimate Value...................... 74

    The Instruction
        Matthew 6:19-34.............. 74

    The Reader: The Instructed............ 80

VII. Actualizing the Ideal..................... 82

    The Instruction
        Matthew 7:1-27.............. 82

    The Reader: The Instructed............ 92

VIII. Modern Disciples and the Sermon........... 94

    A Sermon Summary...................... 95

    Decision and Commitment................ 96

    The Motivation........................ 98

    Implementing the Values.............. 102

Epilogue.. 109

Bibliography.................................... 110

PREFACE

There are many and varied ways to interpret literature, but all worthy literature requires interpretation. It may be interpreted by a reader just being introduced to reading beyond the primer stage, or it may be criticized by the most learned man of letters. For literature was written to be read, and thus interpretation is necessary. Interpretation is absolutely essential if the literary work at hand is to have significant meaning to the reader.

The literature of the Bible has been interpreted for generations by the church and synagogue by methods developed for their own purpose. At times they have neglected the wholeness of the text as well as its literary qualities for the sake of other values. During the eighteenth century there emerged the discipline now called Biblical Criticism whose tack is to develop appropriate methods of studying the Bible. Introductory courses in seminaries and graduate schools of religion give instruction in the interpretation of the Bible. A variety of methods is used, most of which can be brought under the umbrella of Historical Criticism.[1] An impression is often left

---

[1]Edgar Krentz, The Historical-Critical Method (Philadelphia: Fortress Press, 1975), is an excellent summary of this method.

by the method of criticism that the Bible, and especially the Gospels, is a patchwork of isolated segments collected together by a specific writer or group of writers. Since the emergence of redaction criticism, however, there is a tendency to recognize each Gospel as a product of an author who has specific interests and purposes.

In reference to the Gospel of Matthew and the Sermon on the Mount, W. D. Davies has written that "there are documents which are so closely knit that their parts can only be adequately understood in the light of the whole. Such is . . . Matthew."[2] In referring to the Sermon, Davies observes that "the final author of the Gospel, did himself regard v-vii as a unit."[3] In a recent work on Matthew, Peter Ellis reminds us that "the synoptic evangelists were individual theologian-authors who produced properly literary works."[4] Roland Frye has engaged Biblical scholarship by criticizing its methods and calling for

[2]W. D. Davies, The Setting of the Sermon on the Mount (Cambridge: At the University Press, 1966), p. 14.

[3]Ibid., p. 13.

[4]Peter F. Ellis, Matthew, His Mind and Message (Collegeville: The Liturgical Press, 1974), p. v.

the treatment of the Gospels as literary wholes.[5]

It is out of the background of such studies that I have proposed this present work. That is to say, the Gospel of Matthew should be interpreted as a whole and the Sermon as a sub-unit of the whole. I have tried to show in a prior article how the Gospel of Matthew is unified by the design of the authors.[6] I first became impressed with the unity of the thought of the Sermon on the Mount by a series of lectures given by John Wick Bowman in the Spring of 1957 while I was a graduate theological student. This present work will reflect how much I learned from his lectures and subsequently published work, The Sermon From the Mount (Westminster, 1957).

The reader must also be aware that I am writing from a particular vantage point regarding literary criticism. I have been strongly influenced by the new directions in Biblical studies that apply various

[5]Roland Mushat Frye, "A Literary Perspective for the Criticism of the Gospels," Jesus and Man's Hope, eds. Donald G. Miller and Dikran Y. Hadidian (Pittsburg: Pittsburg Theological Seminary, 1971), 193-221; and "The Synoptic Problems and Analogies in Other Literature," The Relationships Among the Gospels, ed. William O. Walker, Jr. (San Antonio: Trinity University Press, 1978), pp. 261-302.

[6]Oscar S. Brooks, "Matthew 28:16-20 and the Design of the First Gospel," Journal for the Study of the New Testament, 10 (January, 1981), 2-18.

literary techniques to the literature of the Bible.[7] Some follow rhetorical criticism. Others talk of narrative criticism, while a few will continue to use the title literary criticism in a very ambiguous way. I have assumed that the final writer of Matthew has composed his Gospel in the form of a narrative. He is telling a story. Whereever and to whomever he is telling it, his intention is to recreate the world of Jesus and his disciples in such a way as to accomplish his goals. As I interpret the Sermon, I try to help the modern reader be sensitive to the relation between the teacher and his disciples as Matthew has portrayed it. That is to say the modern reader must enter, insofar as possible, by his imagination and empathy the world of the disciples. This is the first step in understanding the text.

To follow the newer approaches to Gospel criticism does not displace nor negate prior methods of criticism. It is simply to look at a text from a different point of view. Numerous studies have examined the Sermon on the Mount from the point of view of source, form, redaction criticism, and other methods. I have simply chosen another approach.

------

[7]For a summary of recent developments in Gospel studies cf. R. Alan Culpepper, "Story and History in the Gospels," Review and Expositor, LXXI (1984), 467-478.

Chapter I identifies the wholeness of the Gospel of Matthew and shows how the Sermon is an integral part of its structure. Chapters II-VI interpret the text of the Sermon, Matthew 5-7. At every turn an effort is made to show how each paragraph of the Sermon is related to both the preceding and succeeding paragraphs and builds into a coherent unity. In these central chapters a general plan, with minor variations is followed. (1) Since the author of Matthew sets the Sermon in the mode of a teaching session of Jesus with his disciples, an effort has been made to understand how the disciples heard what Jesus said. As related by Matthew, "What is the message communicated to the disciples by Jesus?" Here is brought to bear the appropriate background and lexical information. (2) A second concern of each chapter is, "How does the contemporary reader read the material?" By approaching the Sermon from these two points of view new insight may be obtained. Throughout the following chapters the various underlying themes in the Sermon are identified. Chapter VII explores how contemporary implementation might be affected. A brief biography of influential works on the Sermon appears at the end of this work.

The primary aim of this work is to write a reasonable interpretation of the Sermon on the Mount as it is given in the Gospel of Matthew. In making this study it appears that the Sermon is ultimately dealing with "Authentic Human Values" and so the sub-title is added. While I accept the final responsibility for the limitation of this work, I must note those who have been of exceptional assistance. Sarah Brooks, my wife, translated the first handscript into typed form. Philip A. Brooks, M.A., my son, has carefully proofread the final copy. Elizabeth Harrison Meloney and Seok Leng Chan have competently and patiently prepared the final copy for publication.

CHAPTER I

THE SERMON
The Ideal Person

"Blessed are the poor in spirit, for theirs is the kingdom of heaven.

"Blessed are those who mourn, for they shall be comforted.

"Blessed are the meek, for they shall inherit the earth.

"Blessed are those who hunger and thirst for righteousness, for they shall be satisfied.

"Blessed are the merciful, for they shall obtain mercy.

"Blessed are the pure in heart, for they shall see God.

"Blessed are the peacemakers, for they shall be called sons of God.

"Blessed are those who are persecuted for righteousness' sake, for theirs is the kingdom of heaven.

Mt. 5:3-10

Jesus' Disciples

"Blessed are you when men revile you and persecute you and utter all kinds of evil against you falsely on my account. Rejoice and be glad, for your reward is great in heaven, for so men persecuted the prophets who were before you.

"You are the salt of the earth; but if salt has lost its taste, how shall its saltness be restored? It is no longer good for anything except to be thrown out and trodden under foot by men.

"You are the light of the world. A city set on a hill cannot be hid. Nor do men light a lamp and put it under a bushel, but on a stand, and it gives light to all in the house. Let your light so shine before men, that they may see your good works and give glory to your Father who is in heaven.

Mt. 5:11-16

The Teacher's Authority

"Think not that I have come to abolish the law and the prophets; I have come not to abolish them but to fulfil them. For truly, I say to you, till heaven and earth pass away, not an iota, not a dot, will pass from the law until all is accomplished. Whoever then relaxes one of the least of these commandments and teaches men so, shall be called least in the kingdom of heaven; but he who does them and teaches them shall be called great in the kingdom of heaven. For I tell you, unless your righteousness exceeds that of the scribes and Pharisees, you will never enter the kingdom of heaven.

Mt. 5:17-20

Ethical Values

1. Human Existence

You have heard that it was said to the men of old, "You shall not kill; and whoever kills shall be liable to judgment." But I say to you that every one who is angry with his brother shall be liable to judgment; whoever insults his brother shall be liable to the council, and whoever says, "You fool!" shall be liable to the hell of fire. So if you are offering your gift at the altar, and there remember that your brother has something against you, leave your gift there before the altar and go; first be reconciled to your brother, and then come and offer your gift. Make friends quickly with your accuser, while you are going with him to court, lest your accuser hand you over to the judge, and the judge to the guard, and you be put in prison; truly, I say to you, you will never get out till you have paid the last penny.

Mt. 5:21-26

2. Sexuality

You have heard that it was said, "you shall not commit adultery." But I say to you that every one who looks at a woman lustfully has already committed adultery with her in his heart. If your right eye causes you to sin, pluck it out and throw it away; it is better that you lose one of your members than that your whole body be thrown into hell. And if your right hand causes you to sin, cut it off and throw it away; it is better that you lose one of your members than that your whole body go into hell.

It was also said, "Whoever divorces his wife, let him give her a certificate of divorce." But I say to you that every one who divorces his wife, except on the ground of unchastity, makes her an adulteress; and whoever marries a divorced woman commits adultery.

Mt. 5:27-32

3. Integrity

Again you have heard that it was said to the men of old, "You shall not swear falsely, but shall perform to the Lord what you have sworn." But I say to you, Do not swear at all, either by heaven, for it is the throne of God, or by the earth, for it is the city of the great King. And do not swear by your head, for you cannot make one hair white or black. Let what you say be simply "Yes" or "No"; anything more than this comes from evil.

Mt. 5:33-37

4. Self-Respect

You have heard that it was said, "An eye for an eye and a tooth for a tooth." But I say to you, Do not resist one who is evil. But if any one strikes you on the right cheek, turn to him the other also; and if any one would sue you and take your coat, let him have your cloak as well; and if any one forces you

to go one mile, go with him two miles. Give to him who begs
from you, and do not refuse him who would borrow from you.

Mt. 5:38-42

5. Love

You have heard that it was said, "You shall love your
neighbor and hate your enemy." But I say to you, Love your
enemies and pray for those who persecute you, so that you may
be sons of your Father who is in heaven; for he makes his sun
rise on the evil and on the good, and sends rain on the just and
on the unjust. For if you love those who love you, what reward
have you? Do not even the tax collectors do the same? And if
you salute only your brethren, what more are you doing than
others? Do not even the Gentiles do the same? You,
therefore, must be perfect, as your heavenly Father is perfect.

Mt. 5:43-48

Motivational Values

1. Almsgiving

Beware of practicing your piety before men in order to
be seen by them; for then you will have no reward from your
Father who is in heaven.

Thus, when you give alms, sound no trumpet before you,
as the hypocrites do in the synagogues and in the streets, that
they may be praised by men. Truly, I say to you, they have
received their reward. But when you give alms, do not let your
left hand know what your right hand is doing so that your alms
may be in secret; and your Father who sees in secret will
reward you.

Mt. 6:1-4

2. Prayer

And when you pray, you must not be like the hypocrites; for they love to stand and pray in the synagogues and at the street corners, that they may be seen by men. Truly, I say to you, they have received their reward. But when you pray, go into your room and shut the door and pray to your Father who is in secret; and your Father who sees in secret will reward you.

And in praying do not heap up empty phrases as the Gentiles do; for they think that they will be heard for their many words. Do not be like them, for your Father knows what you need before you ask him. Pray then like this:

Our Father who art in heaven,

Hallowed be thy name.

Thy kingdom come.

Thy will be done,

On earth as it is in heaven.

Give us this day our daily bread,

And forgive us our debts,

As we also have forgiven our debtors;

And lead us not into temptation,

But deliver us from evil.

For if you forgive men their trespasses, your heavenly Father also will forgive you; but if you do not forgive men their trespasses, neither will your Father forgive your trespasses.

Mt. 6:5-15

3. Fasting

And when you fast, do not look dismal, like the hypocrites, for they disfigure their faces that their fasting may be seen by men. Truly, I say to you, they have received their reward. But when you fast, anoint your head and wash your face, that your fasting may not be seen by men but by your

Father who is in secret; and your Father who sees in secret will
reward you.

Mt. 6:16-18

The Ultimate Value: The Kingdom

Do not lay up for yourselves treasures on earth, where
moth and rust consume and where thieves break in and steal,
but lay up for yourselves treasures in heaven, where neither
moth nor rust consumes and where thieves do not break in and
steal. For where your treasure is, there will your heart be
also.

The eye is the lamp of the body. So, if your eye is sound
your whole body will be full of light; but if your eye is not
sound, your whole body will be full of darkness. If then the
light in you is darkness, how great is the darkness!

No one can serve two masters; for either he will hate the
one and love the other, or he will be devoted to the one and
despise the other. You cannot serve God and mammon.

Therefore I tell you, do not be anxious about your life,
what you shall eat or what you shall drink, nor about your body,
what you shall put on. Is not life more than food, and the body
more than clothing? Look at the birds of the air: they neither
sow nor reap nor gather into barns, and yet your heavenly
Father feeds them. Are you not of more value than they? And
which of you by being anxious can add one cubit to his span of
life? And why are you anxious about clothing? Consider the
lilies of the field, how they grow; they neither toil nor spin; yet
I tell you, even Solomon in all his glory was not arrayed like
one of these. But if God so clothes the grass of the field,
which today is alive and tomorrow is thrown into the oven, will
he not much more clothe you, O men of little faith? Therefore
do not be anxious, saying "What shall we eat?" or "What shall
we drink?" or "What shall we wear?" For the Gentiles seek all
these things; and your heavenly Father knows that you need

them all. *But seek first his kingdom and his righteousness, and all these things shall be yours as well.*

Therefore do not be anxious about tomorrow, for tomorrow will be anxious for itself. Let the day's own trouble be sufficient for the day.

Mt. 6:19-34

Actualizing the Ideal

1. Self-Evaluation

Judge not, that you be not judged. For with the judgment you pronounce you will be judged, and the measure you give will be the measure you get. Why do you see the speck that is in your brother's eye, but do not notice the log that is in your own eye? Or how can you say to your brother, "Let me take the speck out of our eye," when there is the log in your own eye? You hypocrite, first take the log out of your own eye, and then you will see clearly to take the speck out of your brother's eye.

Mt. 7:1-5

2. Discretion

Do not give dogs what is holy; and do not throw your pearls before swine, lest they trample them under foot and turn to attack you.

Mt. 7:6

3. Prayer

Ask, and it will be given you; seek, and you will find; knock, and it will be opened to you. For every one who asks receives, and he who seeks finds, and to him who knocks it will be opened. Or what man of you, if his son asks him for bread, will give him a stone? Or if he asks for a fish, will give him a serpent? If you then, who are evil, know how to give good gifts

to your children, how much more will your Father who is in
heaven give good things to those who ask him! So whatever
you wish that men would do to you, do so to them; for this is
the law and the prophets.

Mt. 7:7-12

4. Choice I

Enter by the narrow gate; for the gate is wide and the
way is easy, that leads to destruction, and those who enter by
it are many. For the gate is narrow and the way is hard, that
leads to life, and those who find it are few.

Mt. 7:13-14

5. Choice II

Beware of false prophets, who come to you in sheep's
clothing but inwardly are ravenous wolves. You will know
them by their fruits. Are grapes gathered from thorns, or figs
from thistles? So, every sound tree bears evil fruit. A sound
tree cannot bear evil fruit, nor can a bad tree bear good fruit.
Every tree that does not bear good fruit is cut down and
thrown into the fire. Thus you will know them by their fruits.

Mt. 7:15-20

6. Choice III

Not every one who says to me, "Lord, Lord," shall enter
the kingdom of heaven, but he who does the will of my Father
who is in heaven. On that day many will say to me, "Lord,
Lord, did we not prophesy in your name, and cast out demons in
your name, and do many mighty works in your name?" And
then will I declare to them, "I never knew you; depart from me,
you evildoers."

Mt. 7:21-23

7. Doing

Every one then who hears these words of mine and does them will be like a wise man who built his house upon the rock; and the rain fell, and the floods came, and the winds blew and beat upon that house, but it did not fall, because it had been founded on the rock. And every one who hears these words of mine and does not do them will be like a foolish man who built his house upon the sand; and the rain fell, and the floods came, and the winds blew and beat against that house, and it fell; and great was the fall of it.

Mt. 7:24-27

CHAPTER II

READING THE SERMON

Any great literature must be read and reread to be understood and appreciated. It must be read for its sentence structure, paragraph structure, smaller and larger contexts, word nuance, imagery, comparisons, contrasts, repetitions, and many other literary features.

So it is with the classic of Jesus' teaching in Matthew 5-7 commonly called The Sermon on the Mount. Not only must the content of the Sermon be studied, but it must be read with an understanding of the complete design of the Gospel as well as its immediate setting in the story that precedes and follows.

The Design of the Gospel[1]

The modern reader will find the clue to the design of the Gospel of Matthew in the concluding paragraph, 28:18-20:

> All authority in heaven and on earth has been given to me. Go therefore and make disciples of all nations, baptizing them in the name of the Father and of the Son and of the Holy Spirit, teaching them to observe all that I have commanded you; and lo, I am with you always, to the close of the ages.

This is a very dramatic scene. It is the only appearance of Jesus to his disciples after his resurrection in the Gospel of Matthew. This intensifies the episode for the reader; whatever else Jesus has done between his resurrection and this moment seems unimportant to the author. The story moves quickly from the resurrection in Jerusalem to a mountain in Galilee, the district where the disciples had received the major part of Jesus' instruction.

---

[1]This section is based on an article by the author, "Matthew 28:16-20 and the Design of the First Gospel," Journal for the Study of the New Testament, 10 (January, 1981), 2-18.

        The content of Jesus' final statement to his
disciples is a commission to them to become involved in
the world mission of his gospel. Jesus begins by
asserting his authority, he then gives the specific
command to make disciples of all people, and ends with
a promise to support them in the enterprise.[2]

        The author had recorded this in an effort to
describe the experience of the original disciples with
the resurrected Lord. By the time the Gospel was
composed, they were already carrying out their
commission. This post-resurrection moment was a
fitting time for them to accept the full authority of
Jesus. They had seen his display of power in his
miracles, as he confronts critics, and now as he
overcomes the power of death. So when Jesus
pronounces, "All authority in heaven and on earth has
been given to me," the disciples understand.
Furthermore, they have been the recipients of numerous
teaching sessions as disciples of the master teacher.
They have learned well their lessons. They know what
it means to be a disciple, a learner, a follower. So
when Jesus commands that his disciples "make
disciples," they understand what it means and that it
includes teaching their disciples what he has taught
them. They can accept the promise that he will be with
them in the future, for they have experienced his
presence in their earthly relation with him. This
concluding paragraph of the Gospel recapitulates the
prior experiences of the original disciples with the
earthly Jesus.

        The author has recorded this final story for
the purpose of inspiring his readers. They are not
eyewitnesses of the ministry of Jesus; they did not
hear his teaching; yet they must not only take his
teaching seriously but also share it with others.
They, too, like the original disciples, must accept the
commission to become involved in the world mission of
the gospel of Jesus.

        The modern reader should look again at Mt.
28:18-20. "Make disciples of all nations," is the

---

[2]Benjamin J. Hubbard, The Matthean Redaction of
a Primitive Apostolic Commissioning: An Exegesis of
Matthew 28:16-20, Society of Biblical Literature
Dissertation Series, Number 19 (Missoula; Scholars
Press, 1974), p. 128.

central clause of the sentence. It is an imperative, a
command. In the original language "make disciples" is
a single word used almost exclusively in Matthew to
describe a learner who receives instruction from one
who is superior in knowledge and authority.[3] This verb
is used to describe both Joseph of Arimathea "who was
discipled to Jesus" (Mt. 27:57) and scribes "who have
been discipled in the Kingdom" (Mt. 13:52). These are
the only three times Matthew has used the verb, and
each time it clearly calls the reader's attention to
the fact that instruction is being transmitted. At the
same time that one is discipled, that is becoming a
disciple, he is preparing to become one who carefully
passes on what he learns. He becomes a transmitter of
tradition which he is taught. All of this takes place
in a unique fellowship with the teacher and their
fellow disciples.

     Further definition to Jesus' central command is
given in the following clauses: baptizing them and
teaching them.   "Baptizing them in the name of . . ."
is a way of saying that the disciple belongs to the one
whose name is mentioned, in this case Jesus, the
Son.[4] As the disciples go out, either the original or
later believers, new disciples will be brought into the
circle of belonging to and fellowship with the master
through the rite of baptism.

     The second clause elaborating the command to
make disciples is so explicit that the reader cannot
miss its importance: "Teaching them to observe all
that I have commanded you." Jesus' commission to his
disciples   that   they   must   make   other   disciples
categorically demands them to teach the new disciples
exactly what Jesus has taught.   This emphasizes the
importance of the teaching of Jesus.   The Gospel of
Matthew alone is explicit in the command to teach.

----

[3]Acts 14:21 is the only place outside of
Matthew the verb appears. Cf. C. K. Rengstorf, TDNT,
IV, p. 416 for definition of "disciple."

[4]Hans Bietenhard, TDNT, V, pp. 245, 268; G.
Adolf Deissman, Bible Studies, trans. Alexander Grieve
(2nd ed.; Edinburg: T & T Clark, 1903), p. 147; James
Hope Moulton and George Milligan, The Vocabulary of the
Greek New Testament (London: Hodder and Stoughton,
Ltd., 1930), onoma (5).

This central command in Mt. 28:18-20 accounts for both the introductory and concluding statements. "All authority in heaven and on earth has been given to me," is the basis of the teaching which the disciples are to communicate to others. At the same time the disciples will draw their own sense of authority and support from this authority, for it becomes the basis of the continued presence of Jesus: "I am with you always."

All of this brings into focus the purpose and design of the entire Gospel. The purpose is to present Jesus as the one endowed with ultimate authority who teaches his disciples the substance of his gospel and inspires them to share it with others. By recording their message the author intends to inspire his readers to participate in the ongoing process of conveying the message from teacher to disciples who in turn convey the message to their disciples in an unbroken tradition. This final paragraph helps the reader discover the design of the Gospel which is structured from beginning to end to emphasize the authority and teaching of Jesus.

The Sermon on the Mount should be read with this in mind. When the reader comes to the concluding paragraph of the Gospel with its claim to authority and its command to make disciples and teach, he cannot avoid recalling that the Sermon began with "his disciples came to him. And he . . . taught them (5:1f.)" and ends with "he taught them as one who had authority (7:29)." The Sermon is a part of that which Jesus commands his disciples to teach--"all that I have comm⁻   :20)." The reader can readily supply the content of "all" by recalling the Sermon and other parts of the Gospel which has been designed to facilitate the transmission of Jesus' teaching.

The Beginning Context: Bethlehem to Capernaum

The Sermon on the Mount must be read with the preceding narrative well in mind. The Gospel opens with a long genealogy designed to connect the following narrative with the past. It is a very impressive list of kings and partriarchs which causes the reader to ask what important character is being introduced. This question is answered partially by the following account of the birth of the one designated by the genealogy. The text describes the miraculous circumstances surrounding the birth of Jesus from the informing of

Joseph to the escape from Herod and the avoiding of
Archelaus. In the account of the birth the reader is
told that this one is the Messiah-King. While his
authority is obvious, the reader wonders: Where is his
kingdom? How will he attain it? How will he rule?

What has been taking place privately in the
birth stories--the beginning of the Messianic era by
the coming of the Messiah--is publicly proclaimed by
John the Baptist as the context for the official
heavenly declaration of the authority of Jesus
(3:17). John's message as presented can be none other
than Messianic. He asserts that there is one coming
after him who is the Messiah. As John makes his
official declaration, Jesus comes to be baptized. It
is at this point that the divine declaration comes to
Jesus. What has been announced about Jesus' authority
is now announced to Jesus. The heavens open, the
Spirit descends, and the voice is heard. The opening
of the heavens indicates that what is about to happen
is coming from the very presence of God. The descent
of the Spirit is a sign of God's appointment. Along
with these the voice identifies Jesus' position of
authority. He is both the Servant of Isaiah (42:1;
61:1-2a) and the King. "Thou art my son" reflects
Ps. 2:7 as well as 2 Sam. 7:14 where the King's
relation to God is that of a son to a father. This
scene is the formal declaration of Jesus' identity. He
stands in a position of authority--Messiah, Son of
Abraham, Son of David, Servant, King. The voice from
heaven climaxes the acclamation of Jesus' authoritative
position being presented in the opening chapters.

The following scene depicts Jesus' confronting
the tempter who subtly refers to Jesus' baptismal
experience by addressing him as the Son of God. The
temptation scene informs the reader that Jesus, whoever
he is or whatever his role, is a definite threat to the
tempter. While the scene impresses the reader with
three things that Jesus will not do, it still leaves
unanswered many questions. For three and one half
chapters the text has related several events about
Jesus. He is identified as an important person, a
Messiah-King, Son of God. He is one with authority.
Yet other questions have not been answered. Where,
when, how will this one establish his kingdom?

From 4:12 the text begins to answer the
reader's questions, at least in part. Whatever Jesus
is going to do will happen when John is put in prison
(4:12), and it will begin in Capernaum (4:13). The

reader is informed that Jesus takes up where John's activity ended. It is at this juncture that the text provides the reader with an emphatic signal that something is about to happen. Verse 17 begins: "From that time Jesus began . . ." The reader will rightly identify "that time" as the imprisonment of John and Jesus' presence in Capernaum. He will further notice that this is a turning point in the narrative since Jesus begins to do something. Now the reader will have an occasion to observe this central character as he shows himself in public. What he does is quite clear. He preaches exactly what John had preached: "Repent, for the kingdom of heaven is at hand." (Cf. 3:2 and 4:17). At this point Jesus has publicly identified himself with a kingdom--it is at hand. It is the same kingdom that John had declared.

On first reading the significance of the phrase "From that time Jesus began to . . ." is not appreciated, but the reader must eventually notice that this precise formula appears here and at only one other point in the Gospel (16:

esus begins his public proclamation. In 16:21 he begins instructing his disciples about his death. So verse 17 informs the reader that the text is at a turning point. It specifies the theme of the preachment, the kingdom of heaven. Furthermore, this preaching of the kingdom is carried by Jesus throughout all Galilee (4:23).

If by this point it has begun to answer some of the questions evoked in the reader about Jesus, the text has also tantalized the reader with a new question--What is the substance of Jesus' sermon about the kingdom? It is at hand. It is the Gospel, the good news, of the kingdom. What does that mean? To answer this question and to resolve many questions about Jesus, the text records a long teaching section, The Sermon on the Mount (5:3-7:28), which is better understood when placed in the context of the preceding narrative which has described Jesus as the King, Messiah, Son, the one with authority. The reader can fit this opening section into the larger design of the Gospel as found in 28:18-20. Jesus, the one with authority, teaches!

The Following Context: From the Mount
of the Sermon to the Mount of Commissioning

The modern reader should not read the Sermon
detached from the subsequent material. The concluding
line of the Sermon, "For he taught them as one who had
authority (7:28)," points to the conclusion of the
Gospel where the themes of teaching and authority
coalesce in the commissioning of the disciples by Jesus
while the theme of authority was already well
established in the opening section of the Gospel. The
Sermon has solidified these two characteristics of
Jesus which continue to be prominent in the remainder
of the Gospel.

As the ministry of Jesus proceeds from the
Sermon on the Mount, the note of authority is always
with him. The term itself appears often as in 8:9;
9:6,8 and 10:1. It is often dramatically presented in
the form of a miracle, it is at times rejected, but
often accepted.

The concentration of miracles in chapters 8 and
9 is an expression of Jesus' authority. The centurion,
a man under authority with authority (8:9), willingly
accepts the authority of Jesus; and a ruler, one in
authority, kneels in recognition of Jesus (9:18).
Jesus' own disciples exclaim: "What sort of man is
this that even winds and sea obey him" (8:27). Jesus
emphatically expresses his authority when he
demonstrates his "authority on earth to forgive
sins . . ." (9:6), and the crowds recognize that the
authority comes from God (9:8). He delegates authority
to his disciples in 10:1.

Jesus' most absolute claim to authority comes
in 11:25-27 where he says "all things have been
delivered to me by my Father." Yet this claim is not
accepted by all, for in the Beelzebul controversy
(12:22-31) Jesus is accused of being in league with the
prince of demons.

In chapter 13 Jesus goes into "his own country"
(13:54) where the people respond to him with
astonishment (13:54), recalling the conclusion of the
Sermon; but at the same time they reject him,
questioning, "Where then did this man get all this?"
(13:56).   The Pharisees continue the rejection of
Jesus' authority as they debate with him (15:1-12), but
the disciples express their acceptance of him when they
confess: "Truly you are the Son of God" (14:33), or
when Peter responds: "You are the Christ" (16:16).

When Jesus moves from Galilee to Jerusalem, the matter of his authority is of immediate concern--"By what authority are you doing these things, and who gave you this authority?" (21:23). This question follows closely the triumphal entry and the cleansing of the Temple, and is asked at a crucial juncture in his ministry. Jesus' answer to this question implies that his authority is from heaven (21:25f). There follows in chapter 22 a series of debates in which the opponents are testing Jesus' authority.

In the closing scenes of the Gospel Jesus is interrogated by the High Priest in terms of his Messiahship (26:63). Pilate questions, "Are you the king of the Jews?" (27:11), and provides his own answer when he placards over the cross, "This is Jesus the king of the Jews" (27:37). Thus the Gospel ends on the same note of authority attributed to Jesus as it begins; for the Magi came asking--"Where is he who has been born king of the Jews?" (2:2).

All of this builds to the final assertion of authority in the closing paragraph of the Gospel. From birth, to crucifixion, from the Mount of the Sermon to the Mount of his appearance, the theme of Jesus' authority is affirmed by the author. It is an emphatic theme. So when the reader comes to the Sermon on the Mount, he must be aware that the one teaching is described throughout as the one with authority.

Likewise, Jesus, the teacher of the Sermon, is pictured as a teacher throughout the Gospel. Soon after the conclusion of the Sermon the text indicates that "Jesus went about all the cities and villages, teaching in their synagogues and preaching the gospel of the kingdom" (9:35 cf. 4:23). The teaching becomes more specific in chapter 10 when Jesus calls his disciples to himself for instructions (10:1) which are finished in 11:1, "and when Jesus had finished instructing his twelve disciples . . ." Later after teaching a series of parables in chapter 13, Jesus asks his disciples if they understand (13:51). It is as if he is asking whether they have learned their lessons. Speaking directly to his disciples, Jesus reminds them that they are being taught as disciples--"Therefore every scribe who has been trained . . ." (13:52). In this particular teaching session Jesus was training his disciples in the same way that he did in the Sermon on the Mount.

Jesus' teaching moves from crowds to disciples and back again. In 15:10 Jesus teaches the crowds and explains things to his disciples (15:15) to whom he gives further instruction concerning his suffering (16:21-23), and they must be faithful in following him (16:24-28). Later an entire chapter (18) is devoted to instructing the disciples about fellowship among themselves.

When Jesus enters Jerusalem, he teaches many parables and enters many debates, and the crowds respond with astonishment. In 23:1-38 the teaching seems to be addressed to the friendly crowds separated from the critics; the audience is further narrowed to his disciples in chapter 24 and concluded by the statement--"and when Jesus had finished all these sayings, he said to his disciples . . ." (26:1).

Again and again the author has reminded the reader that Jesus, a teacher, taught in the presence of crowds--even opponents--as well as his disciples. This contact was important and the Gospel has recorded much of it. All of Jesus' teaching becomes the content of the concluding charge to his disciples--"teaching them to observe all that I have commanded you" (28:20).

From the mount of the Sermon to the mount of his appearance, Jesus is pictured as a teacher. The reader must be aware of this as he considers the Sermon on the Mount. It is not given in isolation but as a part of Jesus' total ministry which is characterized in Matthew by authority and teaching. It is a part of the content implied in the closing commission to the disciples. The author has recorded the Sermon early in his Gospel to inform the reader of Jesus' authoritative teaching. He has kept before the reader this twofold characteristic of Jesus' ministry until the concluding paragraph so the reader will understand that the Sermon is a part of the teaching content commanded by the risen Lord to the world mission of his Gospel.

CHAPTER III

IDEAL DISCIPLES

The Gospel of Matthew methodically introduces the reader to the Sermon. In 4:12 Jesus' moving into public life at the imprisonment of John is accented by the geographical movement from Nazareth to Capernaum so that the prophecy of Isaiah might be fulfilled. It is at this juncture that the text provides the reader with an emphatic signal that something is about to happen. "From that time Jesus began to preach, saying, 'Repent, for the kingdom of heaven is at hand'" (4:17).

Jesus is beginning to preach the good news of the gospel. It is imminent. It attracts great crowds (4:25) and his fame spreads far and wide (4:24). What are the details of this preaching? The reader's curiosity rises and he is anxious to be told.

The specific setting of the Sermon is plotted when Jesus withdraws from the crowds to a mountain where his disciples come to him as he is sitting in lecture fashion. The author has carefully led the reader from a generalized description of Jesus' preaching/healing activities in public places before great crowds to a secluded hillside with his intimate disciples where he teaches them (5:2). The shift of Jesus' audience from crowds to disciples is accompanied by a noticeable change in Jesus' activity. He preached to the crowds, but taught his disciples. This suggests that the situation is more restricted and involves a concern for the details that must be preserved and transmitted. "Teaching" described what a Rabbi did with his disciple students. He instructed them in detailed lessons that they might be prepared to teach others. The author is deliberately describing the intimate session of Jesus with his disciples so that the reader will feel that he is a witness to the first speaking of the Sermon on the Mount.

The Beatitudes: The Ideal Person

The Sermon proper opens with a poem (5:3-10), grammatically in the third person, forming the introduction to the entire teaching. Its poetic form is easily recognized by the casual reader by its parallel construction:

Blessed are the poor in spirit,
    for theirs is the kingdom of heaven.
Blessed are those who mourn,
    for they shall be comforted.
Blessed are the meek,
    for they shall inherit the earth.
Blessed are those who hunger and thirst for
righteousness,
    for they shall be satisfied.
Blessed are the merciful,
    for they shall obtain mercy.
Blessed are the pure in heart,
    for they shall see God.
Blessed are the peacemakers,
    for they shall be called sons of God.
Blessed are those who are persecuted for
righteousness sake,
    for theirs is the kingdom of heaven.

The structure is immediately apparent. The first half of each verse opens with the word "blessed" and states a condition or ideal, and the second half of each verse asserts the benefit or reward. The parallel design is a characteristic feature of Hebrew poetry and would lead to easy presentation and memory in the context of Jesus' teaching. Each verse follows the form: "It's great to be like this, since here is the benefit." The benefit of verses 3 and 10 are the same, giving some reason to consider that this block of verses (3-10) forms a unit.

In addition to the parallel structure, this poem is given in the third person. The intimacy of the personal pronouns "I" and "you" is not felt; instead each line is written in the less personal third person. The speaker's position is not that of an address to someone specific in the audience; rather he seems to be giving a generalized description of an ideal group or company. This third person position gives way in verse eleven to the more intimate "you," and at the same time the parallel in the verses is broken causing the reader to recognize that he is moving into a new section of the Sermon. The form of this unit--its parallelism, use of third person, and beginning and ending verses with identical conclusions--clearly sets it off as an introductory poem to the Sermon.

The first line of each beatitude begins with the word "blessed," a word seldom used in modern English; and modern dictionary definition will not

suffice. In biblical usage it refers to a person who
is fortunate or happy because of a special benefit or
experience. The immediate context almost defines the
word. The blessed person is the one who has received
the benefit; he is the winner; he is fortunate; he is
happy; therefore, he deserves congratulations. So the
entire poem is describing an ideal class of happy or
fortunate people.

They are described by eight characteristics and
eight benefits. The characteristics appear in the
first line of each verse and is slightly more emphatic
in the Greek texts where the first three words are in
the same order in each verse: "Blessed," "the" (plural
in the Greek language), and the characteristic. This
form has a tendency to emphasize the characteristic
even in English translation (brackets identify words
not in Greek text):

        Blessed [are] the poor
        Blessed [are] the mourning [ones]
        Blessed [are] the meek
        Blessed [are] the hungering and thirsting [ones]
        Blessed [are] the merciful
        Blessed [are] the pure [ones] in heart
        Blessed [are] the peacemakers
        Blessed [are] the persecuted [ones]

By defining each of the emphasized terms in the poem
the reader will have a profile of the ideal person or
group being described.

        The poor in spirit. The poor person is one who
has no wealth, goods, or standing in this world. He is
impotent and dependent upon others for his welfare.
"The poor" in the Hebrew Bible certainly refers to
economically impoverished, but they are also identified
as those who recognize that their ultimate salvation
rests with God. The poor was of special concern to God
as evidenced by a prayer for the King of Israel:

        May he judge thy people with righteousness,
            and thy poor with justice!
        ....
        May he defend the cause of the poor of the people,
            give deliverance to the needy,

                                        Ps. 72:2,4

The poor man prayed to God for help:

> This poor man cried, and the Lord heard him;
>   and saved him out of his troubles.
>
>   Ps. 34:6
>
> He raises the poor from the dirt,
>   and lifts the needy from the ash heap.
>
>   Ps. 113:7

The poor realized that their only hope for deliverance was with God. Even in the Hebrew scripture one senses that this dependency is a reference to more than material things, but to make this certain the Sermon adds the word "spirit." The first characteristic of the ideal group being described by Jesus is the recognition of one's spiritual need which only God can meet.

   The ones who mourn. This idea is immediately associated with grief resulting from a personal loss or injury, yet a careful look at the concept of mourning in the Hebrew scripture will show that mourning is a result of sin that has estranged the person or the group from God:

> Comfort, comfort my people,
>   says your God.
> Speak tenderly to Jerusalem,
>   and cry to her
> that her warfare is ended,
>   that her iniquity is pardoned,
> that she has received from the Lord's hand
>   double for all her sins.
>
>   Is. 40:1f.

While the word mourn does not appear here, its implication is obvious. The people are estranged and mourning because of their iniquity which is being removed by the prophetic voice. That mourning precedes restoration with God is further illustrated:

> "Yet even now," says the Lord,
>   "return to me with all your heart,
> with fasting, with weeping, and with mourning;
>   and rend your hearts and not your garments."
> Return to the Lord, your God,
>   for he is gracious and merciful,
> slow to anger, and abounding in steadfast love,
>   and repents of evil.
>   Jl. 2:12f.

In these texts mourning is a result of estrangement and
comfort comes when reconciliation takes place. So the
second characteristic of the ideal group is their
awareness of their estrangement from God and their deep
regret because of it.

          The meek. This characteristic is often
misunderstood because it is too quickly associated with
a mild or withdrawing type person; however, the
biblical personalities described by this term are far
from such an image. Moses is described as "very meek,
more than all men that were on the face of the earth"
(Num. 12:3). Jesus describes himself as such when he
invites people to come to him: "For I am gentle (meek)
and lowly in heart" (Mt. 11:29). While the term "meek"
is used other times in the scriptures, there is no
other occasion where a specific person is described by
the term. Neither Moses nor Jesus were the soft,
unaggressive, withdrawn type. The distinctive
characteristic being described about these two is
understood from reading Psalms 37:

     Trust in the Lord and do good
          so you will dwell in the land and enjoy security.

                         v. 3

     But the meek shall possess the land,
          and delight themselves in abundant prosperity.

                         v. 11

Here trust and meek synonymously describe those who
dwell in the land. Those who trust are meek. They are
willing to depend upon something or someone outside
themselves. Above everything else, the meek person
trusts in God.

          Those who hunger and thirst for
righteousness. The imagery of hungering and thirsting
for God is an accepted imagery in describing the pious
person's desire to be close to God:

     O God, thou art my God, I seek thee,
          my soul thirsts for thee;
     my flesh faints for thee,
          as in a dry and weary land where no water is.

                         Ps. 63:1

As a hart longs
    for flowing streams,
so longs my soul
    for thee, O God.
My soul thirsts for God,
    for the living God.
When shall I come and behold
    the face of God?

Ps. 42:1

In this beatitude, the pious one longs for
righteousness. His desire is to be in the right
relation to God through whatever means are required.
In scripture, Noah is called a righteous man (Gen. 6:9)
because he accepted what was expected of him in
contrast to the evil generation; likewise, Abraham is
accounted righteous, in the right relation to God,
because he responded in faith. This ideal
characteristic identifies the desire for the right
relation to God.

The merciful. This word describes one who
shows compassion and pity toward his fellowman. It is
declared a virtue which God expects of his people:

He has showed you, O man, what is good;
    and what does the Lord require of you
but to do justice, and to love kindness (mercy),
    and to walk humbly with your God?

Mic. 6:8

A dramatic illustration of this characteristic is given
by Jesus in the Parable of the Good Samaritan (Lu.
10:29-37) in which the Samaritan rescues a stranger.
At the conclusion of the parable, the lawyer dialoguing
with Jesus recognizes the Samaritan's action as a deed
of mercy--something that was not forced upon him but
that grew out of the compassion of his heart. So both
the Hebrew scripture and Jesus' own teaching
illustrated that mercy is a virtue pleasing to God.

The pure in heart. The word "heart" refers to
the mind or intellect. What is in one's heart is what
one has in his mind. Thus, it can be the place of
desire and is a definite factor in one's behavior. It
is the place where a person thinks with himself:

> I commune with my heart in the night
> I meditate and search my spirit.
>
> Ps. 77:6

The relation between the heart and action is illustrated:

> Nay, in your hearts you desire wrongs
> your hands deal out violence on earth.
>
> Ps. 58:2

A pure heart, i.e. a proper and sincere mind, fits one to commune with God:

> Who shall ascend the hill of the Lord?
> And who shall stand in his holy place?
> He who has clean hands and a pure heart,
> who does not lift up his soul to what is false,
> and does not swear deceitfully.
>
> Ps. 24:3f.
> (Cf. Ps. 73:1ff.)

"Pure in heart" identifies the characteristic of right mental attitude that relates to behavior.

The peacemakers. This characteristic is stated in an action word. The emphasis is on making peace not simply keeping the peace or having peace of mind. The ideal group described by this word will actively pursue those things that accomplish peace. In the Hebrew scriptures peace encompassed international tranquility, domestic harmony, individual contentment, and a right relation with God:

> and they shall beat their swords into plowshares,
> and their spears into pruning hooks;
> nation shall not lift up sword against nation,
> neither shall they learn war anymore;
> but they shall sit every man under his vine
> and under his fig tree,
> and none shall make them afraid.
>
> Mic. 4:3f.

The peacemaker actively pursues the things that make for peace.

Those who are persecuted for righteousness.
This characteristic is similar to the fourth one which
described the hungering and thirsting ones. In both,
the end or object of concern is righteousness or right
relation to God. In the previous case the ideal group
longs for it; in this case they are willing to be
persecuted for it. This stresses the intense
commitment of those embodying this characteristic; they
are willing to suffer personally on behalf of their
relation to God.

These are the eight characteristics that
introduce the Sermon on the Mount. They are terms
representing the best piety of the religious tradition
of Jesus' day. Those who possess these characteristics
are very fortunate, for they enjoy certain benefits
which are stated in the second half of each verse.
They may be listed:

        the kingdom is theirs
        they shall be comforted
        they shall inherit the earth
        they shall be satisfied
        they shall obtain mercy
        they shall see God
        they shall be called sons of God
        the kingdom is theirs

This simple listing graphically emphasizes that the
kingdom is the benefit granted. It appears first and
last, and is a present possession. The present tense
is must be emphasized; and the first and last lines are
better translated: "the kingdom of heaven is
theirs." This phrasing accentuates that they possess
citizenship in the kingdom or they are already
participating in the kingdom. This is an unusual idea
since the traditional concept of Jesus' day held the
kingdom of heaven in the future when the fortunes of
Israel would be restored. In the first and last
benefit "the kingdom" stands as the subject of the
sentence and "theirs" completes the thought. This
change in form emphasizes the importance of the
kingdom.

In contrast, lines two through seven have some
aspect of the ideal people for the subject and the
thought is completed by identifying the benefit. At
the same time the enjoyment of the benefit is postponed
into the future. The text is intentionally
establishing a contrast, tension, or paradox for the
reader. This is further compounded when it is realized

that these benefits are the blessings usually
anticipated in the future kingdom. The text is
affirming that the kingdom of heaven with its ideal
participants is a present reality. There are already
those who are participating in its benefits, but the
blessings are not exhausted, for there is more to come.

When the entire eight beatitudes are taken
together, it will be noted from the above listing of
benefits that all characteristics and benefits are
bracketed by "The kingdom of heaven is theirs." The
structure of this opening poem contributes to the
emphasis that it is a generalized description of those
ideal people who participate in the kingdom. The first
and last verses of the poem speak of the "poor in
spirit" and "those who are persecuted for
righteousness." These two ideas are complementary.
The "poor" person recognizes that his total dependency
is upon God with whom he desires the right
relationship; and he is willing to be involved no
matter what the cost might be--even persecution.
Included between these two complementary poles are six
characteristics and blessings.

The first four beatitudes may be taken together
as a description of the inner spiritual disposition of
the ideal pious person. He depends upon God, he mourns
because of his estrangement, he is willing to trust,
and he longs for a right relationship. This direction
of interpretation can be expanded to describe the
spiritual pilgrimage or religious experience typical of
one's becoming involved with the kingdom. Parallel to
this would be the interpretation of the second four
beatitudes as inner characteristics that eventually
express themselves in outward action to or for one's
fellowman. Mercy, purity of heart as related to
conduct, and peacemaking are of little consequence if
only an inner attitude. They must be expressed. To
follow this line of interpretation will certainly bring
to light the inner and outer nature of the ideal being
described in the introductory poem. While this helps
the reader gain an insight into the text, he would not
wish to stop at this point since there are other
overtones to be found in the poem.

There are at least five contrasting themes in
this opening paragraph. (1) The contrast of the
inner/outer as just described. (2) This might also be
called the reflective/action theme, for these eight
characteristics indicate such. Poor in spirit,
mourning, meek, merciful, and purity of heart will

eventually lead to action along with peacemakers. (3)
The heavenly/earthly or this world/other world is
another contrasting theme. The kingdom of heaven is a
felt reality but some will inherit the earth. It is on
this earth, this world, that the ideal ones will be
persecuted. (4) The God/man relation is obvious. Man
longs for God's righteousness. Man desires God's mercy
and hopes to become sons of God. All of this assumes
that there is an ideal relation between God and man.
(5) The man/man relation is present. Man must
mercifully seek to make peace with his fellowman
through appropriate conduct. Man desires this harmony
along with appropriate harmony with God.

        Jesus, in the text of the Sermon, begins with a
paragraph--a poem--that describes people. Whether
individually or collectively, the description is given
in the plural in a generalized fashion about non-
specific people. He is describing an ideal in terms
easily recognized and understood by his disciples, for
his language and ideas were a part of the best
religious piety of his day. He has given a list of
distinctive qualities describing the disposition or
characteristic of the ideal ones who participate in the
kingdom. Whatever Jesus has said prior to this
teaching about the Gospel of the kingdom, he now begins
to give definition to that idea as he lists these
characteristics. At the same time he has introduced at
least five themes that will recur throughout the
Sermon. This paragraph has been presented in brief
poetic fashion making it easy to memorize and retain as
the basis for further reflection.

        The reader must accept the poetic nature of
this opening paragraph and avoid a method of
application that dissects the poem. While the text is
describing the ideal participant in the kingdom, it
should not be segmented or categorized to find eight
and only eight characteristics of the true believer.
Rather the poem should be used in a wholistic
fashion. The believer, or participant, has a
distinctive disposition. Here are eight facets of that
person's disposition. They may overlap, and they may
be expanded, but certainly the whole of the disposition
does not equal the parts. This would be an unworthy
mechnical definition. Yet the profile of the ideal
person begins to emerge: He is one who has had a deep
and abiding experience of his own inadequacy, which
experience has led him to an inner desire to have the
right relation to God, and his fellowman.

Salt and Light: Jesus' Disciples

The poem is part of the introduction, and the reader must await the body of the Sermon for the full development of the ideas present here. A second brief section of the introduction comes in 5:11-16:

"Blessed are you when men revile you and persecute you and utter all kinds of evil against you falsely on my account. Rejoice and be glad, for your reward is great in heaven, for so men persecuted the prophets who were before you.

"You are the salt of the earth; but if salt has lost its taste, how can its saltness be restored? It is no longer good for anything except to be thrown out and trodden under foot by men."

"You are the light of the world. A city set on a hill cannot be hid. Nor do men light a lamp and put it under a bushel, but on a stand, and it gives light in the house. Let your light so shine before men, that they may see your good works and give glory to your Father who is in heaven."

If the lofty ideals of the generalized poem might seem out of the disciples' reach, Jesus, as the text proceeds, draws them into the atmosphere of the Sermon by addressing them directly. Verse 11 abruptly changes from the impersonal third person to the more intimate "you" which is used throughout the remainder of the Sermon until the closing paragraphs.

"Blessed are you . . ." addresses the disciples specifically and provides the transition by retaining the word "blessed" as well as applying the last verse of the poem about persecution to them. Jesus is explicitly asserting his confidence that the disciples are committed to the profile just described and that their loyalty can and will stand up under persecution. While the object of loyalty and the cause of persecution were righteousness in the poem, vv. 11-12 have shifted the focus to Jesus himself, ". . . on my account." This identifies the disciples' commitment, not with some abstraction about the heavenly kingdom, but rather with the person Jesus, who speaks to them. This again emphasizes the personal and intimate turn of the Sermon and its application to the disciples. In their loyalty to Jesus they are like the divine spokesmen, prophets of old, who participated with God in bringing his message to the world.

The importance of loyal disciples committed to

the person of Jesus and God's message is elaborated by
the use of the imagery of salt and light. The text
quotes Jesus' very emphatic assertion to the
disciples: "You are the salt of the earth" (v. 13).
The essential nature of salt has been recognized by
mankind throughout history, for without it man cannot
survive. So a simple reading of the image will produce
a reasonable meaning; however, the word "earth"
stimulates an inquiry since it may be a reference to
the planet earth, or it may be contrasted with "world"
when "world" is a reference to the sum total of the
universe and "earth" refers only to soil. If the
latter is the case, then the assertion is "you, my
disciples, are salt for the soil." This is a fitting
application for salt when it is recalled that salt was
used as a stimulant/fertilizer in agriculture in Jesus'
day. Contrary to modern production, the salt of Jesus'
day could lose its saltness as the sodium chloride was
leached out leaving a residue resembling gypsum.[1] Thus
in this introductory section the disciples are being
instructed in their duty. As ideal, committed
followers, they will stimulate productivity in others
or else they will be useless.

"You are the light of the world" (v. 14).
"Light" may call forth exaggerated imagination of all
the luminaries that fill the heavens and spread their
rays throughout the universe, yet the context here
describes "light" in its immediate and practical use.
It is used as a means of dispelling the night darkness
so that man can continue with needed affairs. The
disciples have an important possession that is as
useful to their fellowman as light in a darkened town
or home. Their role is to display it so that their
fellowman will recognize its unique value and give
honor, not to the disciples, but to God in heaven.

These three brief paragraphs in this second
section of the introduction have drawn the disciples
into the center of the teaching and have identified
their positive loyalty to Jesus. It has been made
quite clear to them that their disposition will indeed
evoke the attention of their fellowman. At times they
may be persecuted, but they are not to despair, for

---

[1]Eugene P. Deatrick, "Salt, Soil, Savior,"
Biblical Archaeologist, XXV (1962), 41-48.

they have blessings to share with others which are as
essential to the survival of humankind as salt or
light. They will stimulate growth in others. They
have not only been exposed to Jesus' generalized ideal,
but they have been briefed on how the ideal must be
operative in their lives.

Many of the five contrasting themes may be
found in this paragraph. The disciples, persecuted on
earth, have their reward in heaven. They will produce
good works, action, in such a way that God's man will
be honored by men. Their inner disposition is taking
outward expression.

The Reader: One of the Disciples

The sensitive reader can detect that the gospel
has been composed in a way not only to draw the
disciple into the intimacy of Jesus' teaching but also
to bring the reader into the circle of instruction.
When Jesus begins the Sermon he withdraws from the
crowds and his disciples come to him (5:1). The
teaching session puts the reader in the position of one
who is listening to a private teaching by Jesus; but
then the Sermon begins with a very generalized
description of the ideal disciple, leaving open the
possibility that the reader will vicariously join the
teaching session. As he listens, the reader soon hears
Jesus address him specifically: "Blessed are you" . .
. "You are the salt" . . . "You are the light . . ."
In this unusual manner the reader becomes one of the
disciples as he listens to the teaching of Jesus. This
is an ingenius device of the author recording the
Sermon.

What then has the reader learned from the first
section of the Sermon on the Mount?

1.   He has learned that "kingdom of heaven,"
"righteousness," and "on my (Jesus') account" are all
bound up together. The right relation to God and the
right relation to Jesus are brought together as
synonymous blessings.   Insofar as the kingdom is
present, Jesus is bringing about the conditions in
which one becomes a part of it. The kingdom of heaven,
however it will be further defined, is that condition
of being in the proper relation to God as described in
Jesus' teaching.

2.   The reader is aware that the ideal disciple
described by Jesus has experienced a religious

awakening in his inner disposition that has identified
his utter dependency upon God. The eight beatitudes
have amply described the dynamic characteristics of the
committed disciple. Exactly what set in motion the
inner feeling that brings the disciple to this
conclusion is not detailed, yet "spiritually poverty
stricken" and "mourner" suggest the beginning point of
the pilgrimage. This will be further resolved in the
body of the Sermon.

3. The reader knows that Jesus' teaching is not
instruction in only the inner life of contemplation,
but the life of the disciple must affect the affairs of
his fellowman. The new disposition may simply be
noticed because of the countenance of the disciple, but
that is not enough. There will be good works honoring
God, growing out of the disciples' commitment.

4. Even in this brief introduction, the reader
discovers that true disciples will suffer. This will
result from his bipolar relations. On the one hand he
is committed to a heavenly kingdom where abide his
ultimate blessings, but he is inspired to implement his
heavenly vision in the here and now of his earthly
existence.

5. The reader concludes this section desiring
more. He wants to be instructed how to relate to his
fellowman, how to relate to God, and more guidance in
how to develop that utter dependency that brings
himself into a harmonious relation with God. This he
will learn from the remainder of the Sermon.

CHAPTER IV

ETHICAL VALUES

Turning from a general description of the ideal disciple, the Sermon proceeds to discuss specific areas of a disciple's thought and action. Jesus' teaching will deal with such ancient laws as murder, adultery, oaths, and retaliation and make fitting application for his disciples. Before explaining and elaborating how the characteristics of the ideal disciple are expressed or implemented, the text will deal with the matter of the rights of the teacher, Jesus.

The Teacher: His Authority

This new section of the Sermon begins with Jesus' own declaration of authority, his relation to the scriptures, and other teachers or groups of the day. He asserts the importance of his own commandments:

Think not that I have come to abolish the law and the prophets; I have come not to abolish them but to fulfill them. For truly, I say to you, till heaven and earth pass away, not an iota, not a dot, will pass from the law until all is accomplished. Whoever then relaxes one of the least of these commandments and teaches men so, shall be called least in the kingdom of heaven; but he who does them and teaches them shall be called great in the kingdom of heaven. For I tell you, unless your righteousness exceeds that of the scribes and Pharisees, you will never enter the kingdom of heaven.

Mt. 5:17-20

Beginning with this paragraph and continuing through the body of the Sermon, the personal pronoun "I" is emphasized along with "you": "I say to you . . ." appears repeatedly in an authoritative and demanding manner to emphasize the importance of the teaching. This has the effect of making the teaching setting even more intimate. Jesus is speaking directly to the band of disciples assembled on the mountain in Galilee.

In the text, Jesus begins by denying any intention of abrogating the sacred writings of the

Hebrews, but he declares his right to fulfill them (v. 17). "To fulfill" means "to make complete" or "to clarify the true meaning of."[1] This is what Jesus does in the subsequent paragraphs when he says, "you have heard it said of old . . . but I say unto you . . ." He states a law from the Old Testament and then proceeds to give his expanded interpretation of it. Thus he not only fulfills the law but also displays his authority to do so, and at the same time makes it binding on his disciples.

Jesus' dedication to the law is further emphasized in the following sentence of verse 18 where he insists that the law is as eternal as heaven and earth, and it will all be eventually clarified. In fact, that is exactly what the text will do in the succeeding sections. Verse 18 is parallel and repetitious to verse 17:

17a Think not that I have come to abolish
    the law and the prophets.
18a Till heaven and earth pass away not an
    iota, not a dot will pass from the law.
17b I have come not to abolish them but to
    fulfill them.
18b Until all is accomplished.

While he recognizes and accepts the importance of the law, Jesus calls attention to the fact that the law will be completed and proceeds to reinterpret and/or modify its significance and application; thus, the law is relative in importance to his teaching. Verse 19 makes this explicit.

"These commandments" is a reference to the teachings that are to follow. They are authoritative demands on the life of the disciple; and his response to them will demonstrate the quality of his righteousness--his right relation to God; and his response determines his position in the kingdom of heaven. This is repeated three times in vv. 19f: "least in the kingdom," "greatest in the kingdom," and "never enter the kingdom of heaven."

---

[1]W. F. Albright and C. S. Mann, Matthew, The Anchor Bible (New York: Doubleday & Company, Inc., 1971), p. 58.

The ideal disciple who longs for a right relation with God, i.e. who longs to be a part of the kingdom, is now told that he must give evidence of obeying Jesus' commandments, his clarifying and completing the Old Testament laws, which follow. By following Jesus' instructions the disciples will go beyond the practices of the scribes and Pharisees (5:20). This urgency to obedience is further articulated at the end of the Sermon when Jesus concludes: "Every one then who hears these words of mine and does them is like a wise man . . ." Thus between two demands for a positive response, at the beginning (5:17-20) and at the end (7:24ff) of the Sermon, Jesus elaborates the precepts that amplify the characteristics of the ideal disciple described in 5:13-16. This note of authority further reflects the concluding commission to the disciples in 28:16-20: ". . . teaching them to observe all that I have commanded you." Thus 5:17-20 becomes the authoritative premise on which the remainder of the Sermon is based.

The Instruction: Ethical Values

Human beings often conduct their lives on a system of rules that tell them what is right and wrong. The rule tells us not to take a toy away from baby brother, to tell the truth to the teacher, not to cheat on a test, or not to steal from a neighbor. To make a list of all the rules that we use would exhaust many pages of writing and create a cumbersome array of "do's" and "don'ts," yet they seem necessary to human life and assist in the orderly course of society.

The person who reflects upon all the rules of life will discover that they can very easily be grouped in umbrella categories which can be called moral principles or values. A moral value is a broad, general concept that identifies a worth or priority. It designates something that is worth preserving. Values become the basic system of priorities on which the rules are based. For example, society has a set of rules governing the operation of motor vehicles. These rules are designed to facilitate the flow of traffic on our streets and highways and at the same time preserve human life. That is to say rules of automobile safety have developed out of the values society holds dear. The list of values that one might produce as the broad categories for a system of rules would be few in number.

At the same point in one's considering rules and values he may ask the question: "Why be moral?" "Why assent to values?" "Why obey the rules?" At this point he is probing the presuppositions on which morality is based. He is searching for the authority that validates the values and confirms the worthiness of the priorities. These three categories identify the different levels at which a discussion of right and wrong, values and priorities, and the why of it all can be carried out. (1) What are the rules? (2) What are the values? (3) Why be moral?

In the Sermon on the Mount the text deals primarily with (2) and (3). In the sections covered by Mt. 5:3-20 question (3) has been addressed. One will have values and be moral because he has come into the right relation to God and his kingdom as he relates to Jesus and his teaching. The disciple has experienced estrangement and reconciliation (5:3-6) and has become a son of God (5:9), a son who is willing to be noticed and persecuted (5:11-16). He has had a religious experience which indelibly identifies him with Jesus whose authority he accepts. Since the disciples have come into a right relation to God through Jesus, it is reasonable that they would accept his assertion of authority to teach them (5:17-20). This will answer the why question for the disciples. They accept the authority of Jesus because he has led them into a right relation with God.

Values, the second level of a moral discussion, is the matter of the remainder of this chapter. Beginning in 5:21 Jesus carefully articulates five significant values for the life of the disciples. This section (5:21-48) forms a definite unit in which each of the five paragraphs follow a fixed structure beginning with the catch phrase, "You have heard that it was said . . . but I say to you . . ." Each paragraph begins with a former law which is reinterpreted or modified by Jesus. It is then amplified and concluded with a statement of the seriousness of the matter. These paragraphs reflect the Beatitudes and identify a specific value being proposed by the Sermon. These values cover the widest possible spectrum of humnan existence and can be listed as follows: (1) the value of human existence, (2) the value of sexuality, (3) the value of personal integrity, (4) the value of self-respect, and (5) the value of love. The form and content of 5:21-48 have been outlined in figure 1.

Figure 1

FORM AND CONTENT OF MATTHEW 5:21-48

	I Former Law	II Modification	III Amplification	IV Seriousness	V Value	VI Beatitude
(1)	21-26 You shall not kill	Anyone who is angry is liable	If you are at altar ... leave be reconciled	Never get out till you have paid ...	Respect for human existence	Blessed are the merciful
(2)	27-32 You shall not commit adultery	Who looks at a woman lustfully ... adultery	Pluck out eye cut off hand	Better lose one member than whole body	Respect for sexuality	Blessed are the merciful/ pure in heart
				Everyone who divorces ... whoever marries	Adultery: A breach of the modified rule	
(3)	33-37 You shall not swear falsely	Do not swear at all	Not by heaven, earth Jerusalem head	Anything more than yes or no is evil	Concern for integrity	Blessed are the pure in heart
(4)	38-42 An eye for eye	Do not resist one who is evil	Strike, sue, forces to go one mile, give, do not refuse		Proper, self-respect	Blessed are the peace-makers
(5)	43-47 You shall love neighbor, hate enemy	Love your enemies	Love like God not like Gentiles	You may be sons of God	Summary	Peacemakers committed to righteous-ness

The value of human existence is introduced by a
discussion of the Old Testament law against murder.

> You have heard that it was said to the men of
> old, 'You shall not kill; and whoever kills shall
> be liable to judgment.' But I say to you that
> every one who is angry with his brother shall be
> liable to judgment; whoever insults his brother
> shall be liable to the council, and whoever says,
> 'You fool!' shall be liable to the hell of fire.
> So if you are offering your gift at the altar, and
> there remember that your brother has something
> against you, leave your gift there before the altar
> and go; first be reconciled to your brother, and
> then come and offer your gift. Make friends
> quickly with your accuser, while you are going with
> him to court, lest your accuser hand you over to
> the judge, and the judge to the guard, and you be
> put in prison; truly, I say to you, you will never
> get out till you have paid the last penny.

Mt. 5:21-26

"You shall not kill" is a direct quotation from Ex.
20:13, the sixth of the Ten Commandments. "And whoever
kills shall be put to death." Jesus deals with this
subject not because the Hebrews lacked an appreciation
for life, for throughout their history the commandment
and the later commentary taught that life is sacred to
God. The creation story recognizes that life has come
from God: "Let us make man in our image . . . so God
created man in his own image" (Gen. 1:26f.); and God
punished the first person to commit homicide (Gen. 4:8-
16). So there is an adequate foundation in the society
of Jesus' day for an understanding of the worth of
human existence.

In this text Jesus goes beyond the expressions
of his day by insisting that one becomes "liable" not
just for what he does but for his attitude. This is
emphasized in three parallel statements:

> If one is angry with his brother...
>   liable ... to judgment
> If one insults his brother...
>   liable ... to council
> If one says 'you fool!'...
>   liable ... to hell of fire

The three expressions against the brother is not a list
of specific words to avoid but rather descriptive of an

unacceptable attitude of a disciple toward his fellowman. In general, anger is feeling aroused out of unfortunate circumstances that leads to evil. James 2:20 notes that "The anger of man does not work the righteousness of God," and a second-century writer said that anger leads to murder (Didache 3:2). Anger is a reaction against another human being who, it is judged, has violated one's rights; therefore, he deserves to be punished. It is the first step in mistreating a fellowman.

The word translated "insults" is a word of abuse. It degrades one's fellowman by referring to him as empty-headed. The same is true of "fool." It verbally degrades a person by describing him as foolish and stupid. All three of these words are expressions of the speaker's disregard for the nobler aspects of human life and his effort to demean the person spoken about. The speaker is implying that the person is lower than himself and stands in an inferior and unworthy position in society.

This is an unacceptable attitude toward one's fellowman and is vigorously condemned by the liability expressed. A person guilty of such an attitude deserves to be judged himself, even by the most respected council of the day--the Jewish Sanhedrin in Jerusalem; nor is any punishment too severe--not even the eternal fire of hell! In this text, for Jesus, the disciple's attitude toward his fellowman is of the utmost consequence; for it represents the disciples' worth of human life--the value of human existence. This represents a significant shift of emphasis from the former law and Jesus' restatement. The former emphasized restraint and punishment for a wrong act while Jesus focuses on the inner attitude of the disciple. This emphasis will be retained throughout the remainder of the Sermon.

The seriousness of maintaining the proper attitude toward the worth of human life is further emphasized by reminding the disciples that they cannot be in harmony with God when they are out of harmony with their fellowman. So worship at an altar--an effort to communicate and establish a right relation with God--is useless until the appropriate attitude/relationship is established with the wronged brother. The last two verses (25f) of this paragraph reminds the disciples that delay in correcting a wrong attitude complicates and compounds the wrong.

Jesus has begun with an ancient law and modified it to emphasize the inner disposition of the disciple. He will have a positive, wholesome attitude toward his fellowman. He will not degrade him by abusive thoughts expressed in unkind language, for every man is a worthy creation of God. This is dealing with a basic value or priority for the disciple's conduct. The disciple must always act on the basis of the value of human life.

The value of sexuality naturally follows the discussion of respect for human existence. Life itself is dependent upon the appropriate relation of man and woman; and many of the social activities, customs, and taboos focus on the male/female relationship. The fact that societies, both ancient and modern, have developed elaborate codes regulating the conduct of the opposite sexes towards each other demonstrates that mankind has always recognized the importance of human sexuality.

The ideal relation between male and female is addressed by Jesus in Mt. 19:5f.: "'For this reason a man shall leave his father and mother and be joined to his wife, and the two shall become one flesh?' So they are no longer two but one flesh." Jesus quotes and approves Gen. 2:24 which is the conclusion to the story of God's creating a partner for Adam because God said, "It is not good that man should be alone" (Gen. 2:18). So he created for Adam a "helper"--one who can communicate, respond, and dialogue with another.[2] This new creation is woman, the opposite sex. It was the Creator's design that human existence would be of greater value by having human beings of the opposite sex. Thus by design the value of human sexuality stands along side the value of human existence in importance.

In the Sermon, Jesus discusses the ideal relation of the sexes under the laws of adultery and divorce.

You have heard that it was said, "You shall not commit adultery." But I say to you that every one

---

[2]Cf. Helmut Thielicke, The Ethics of Sex, trans. John W. Doberstein (Grand Rapids: Baker Book House, 1964), pp. 4f.

who looks at a woman lustfully has already
committed adultery with her in his heart. If your
right eye causes you to sin, pluck it out and throw
it away; it is better that you lose one of your
members than that your whole body be thrown into
hell. And if your right hand causes you to sin,
cut it off and throw it away; it is better that you
lose one of your members than that your whole body
go into hell.

Mt. 5:27-30

"You shall not commit adultery" is the seventh
Commandment, regulating the relation between the
opposite sexes. It follows immediately the ban against
murder; and Jesus retains the same sequence here, again
demonstrating the inter-relatedness of the two ideas.
Adultery in the Old Testament was punishable by death
of either or both partners in the affair (Dt. 22:22-
29). In the case-law statements about adultery, the
male is described as the one taking the initiative. He
perpetrates the act against the woman, yet the wronged
person is described as the husband of the wife. The
man committing adultery shall be executed because he
violated his neighbor's wife (Dt. 22:24). The sin was
against the neighbor. That is because in the society
of Jesus' day and earlier women were considered in the
care of first their father who protected their
virginity and then their husband who protected their
faithfulness from unworthy males. So the honor of a
father or husband was violated if the daughter or wife
were mistreated. This placed the woman in a position
of secondary consideration.[3] Yet the ban on adultery
was designed to preserve respect for the opposite
sex. Sexual intercourse was not to be used by male or
female for momentary, personal satisfaction outside the
marriage relationship and the regulation of the
community. Such restrictions were designed to prevent
a person or persons from being used as objects of
gratification rather than partners in an ongoing
fellowship. Such action was a violation of the
Creator's design--that is adultery!

---

[3]For a complete description of the position of
women in Hebrew society cf. Roland de Vaux, Ancient
Israel: Its Life and Institutions, trans. John McHugh
(London: Darton, Longman and Todd, 1961), pp. 19-40.

When Jesus modifies the original law, he is making an effort to establish respect for the opposite sex at the level of inner appreciation rather than just the outward act: "Every one who looks at a woman lustfully has already committed adultery with her in his heart."   This is a drastic accusation against the one who lustfully desires the sexual pleasures of another; yet is in keeping with the tone of the Sermon; for, if anger is a violation of the law against murder, then lust violates the law against adultery.   The thought begins to make an object for self-gratification of the other person rather than one for whom sincere respect is due.   Jesus' comment does not specify the status of the woman being contemplated; whether the woman is married, betrothed (engaged), or a young virgin is not made known.   The wrong is the same in any situation.   The serious nature of such thoughts were noted by other teachers in Judaism.   One Rabbi said: "If one gazes lustfully at the little finger of a woman, it is as if he gazed at her [private parts]."[4]

Jesus continues to emphasize the severity of the sin when he prescribes the corrective: "If your right eye causes you to sin pluck it out . . . better . . . lose one of your members than . . . whole body thrown into hell."   As with the sin of anger, so with the sin of evil thought, the logical punishment is hell.   This augments the seriousness of the inner thoughts.   The first part of the sentence about plucking out the eye seems ironic if put into practice. If every evil thought was followed by an act of self-mutilation, how long would a human being survive?   Better to take the statement as an hyperbole demanding that appropriate and decisive action be taken as soon as a lustful thought is identified.[5]

Beginning with an Old Testament law Jesus has raised the question of the relation of male and female. He discusses the value of human sexuality. He impresses upon his disciples the necessity of appropriate thought or right inner attitude toward the opposite sex, for it is within the heart of man that evil is devised--"Blessed are the pure in heart."

---

[4]Quoted by Albright, op. cit., p. 63.

[5]Dt. 25:11f. prescribes the cutting off of one's hand as punishment for a specific wrong act.

In this teaching on the value of human sexuality a concern for the treatment of the woman is accentuated. In v. 28 "with her" calls attention to the fact that the wrong is against the woman rather than just her husband. To further elaborate this concern, Jesus introduces the subject of divorce.

It was also said, "Whoever divorces his wife, let him give her a certificate of divorce." But I say to you that every one who divorces his wife, except on the ground of unchastity, makes her an adulteress; and whoever marries a divorced woman commits adultery.

Mt. 5:31-32

For many generations divorce had been practiced in Hebrew tradition. The basis for it was codified in the laws of Deuteronomy.

When a man takes a wife and marries her, if then she finds no favor in his eyes because he has found some indecency in her, and he writes her a bill of divorce and puts it in her hand and sends her out of his house, and she departs out of his house, and if she goes and becomes another man's wife, and the latter husband dislikes her and writes her a bill of divorce and puts it in her hand and sends her out of his house, or if the latter husband dies, who took her to be his wife, then her former husband, who sent her away, may not take her again to be his wife, after she has been defiled; for that is an abomination before the Lord, and you shall not bring guilt upon the land which the Lord your God gives you for an inheritance.

Dt. 24:1-4

The ambiguity of "some indecency" caused no little discussion among the interpreters of this code, even in Jesus' day. The Mishnah makes clear the wide range of interpretation for grounds for divorce.

The School of Shammai say: A man may not divorce his wife unless he has found unchastity in her, for it is written, Because he hath found in her indecency in anything. And the School of Hillel say: [He may divorce her] even if she spoiled a dish for him, for it is written, Because he hath found in her indecency in anything.

R. Akiba says: Even if he found another fairer
than she, for it is written, <u>And it shall be if she
find no favour in his eyes</u> . . .

Gittin 9:10[6]

Both the <u>Mishnah</u> and the book of Deuteronomy record
that the divorce proceeding was the privilege of the
husband, and the wife had little recourse.   As time
went by women gained the privilege of initiating
divorce as attested by a document from the second
century A.D.[7]   Modern readers may rightfully wonder
whether women suffered under the rules of divorce.

Jesus' modification of the law of divorce is
consistent with his remark in Mt. 19:8 where he
explains that the law of Moses permitted divorce
because the people by the hardness of their hearts were
rejecting the original intention of the Creator that
marriage was a covenant not to be broken.   The prophet
Malachi had reiterated this demand generations before.

And this again you do.   You cover the Lord's
altar with tears, with weeping and groaning because
he no longer regards the offering or accepts it
with favor at your hand.   You ask, "Why does he
not?" Because the Lord was witness to the covenant
between you and the wife of your youth, to whom you
have been faithless, though she is your companion
and your wife by covenant.   Has not the one God
made [has he not made one] and sustained for us the
spirit of life?   And what does he desire?   Godly
offspring.   So take heed to yourselves, and let
none be faithless to the wife of his youth.   "For I
hate divorce, says the Lord the God of Israel, and
covering one's garment with violence, says the Lord
of hosts.   So take heed to yourselves and do not be
faithless.

Mal. 2:13-16

---

[6]Quoted from <u>The Mishnah</u>, trans. Herbert Danby
(Oxford: University Press, 1933) is the compilation of
oral law made near the end of the second century A.D.

[7]de Vaux, op. cit., p. 35.

So in banning divorce Jesus is simply recovering the
original intention of the appropriate relation of the
opposite sexes in marriage. The intensity of the wrong
of divorce is identified when it is said that the one
divorcing his wife "makes her an adultress." She is
now guilty of breaking the commandment "Thou shalt not
commit adultery." She stands in the same position as a
wife who willingly has met her paramour in illicit sex
and has been discovered. She has violated the marriage
and, according to the law, deserves to be executed.
The husband who divorced her has done this to her.
Having been divorced, the woman's position in society
is the same as an unmarried woman who has wrongfully
given up her virginity. In this modification of the
law of divorce, Jesus places the husband in the role of
one who has illicitly assumed the privilege of sex with
a woman. This wrong action not only affects husband
and wife, but it also potentially disrupts the
community by involving another man who might want to
marry the divorced wife. He too will be caught up in
the violation of the marriage covenant.

The only concession in this rather rigorous
teaching is a reference to the woman's "unchastity."
The husband's action is justified only if it is evident
that the wife has been unfaithful. Modern interpreters
will debate whether Jesus actually said this or it has
been added by those passing on the teaching of
Jesus.[8] The presence or absence of this clause in the

---

[8]The argument proceeds from the fact that in
these five paragraphs in Mt. 5:21-48 there are no
exceptions to the absolute demands of Jesus except
here. Since this breaks the pattern, it was not
original with Jesus. This may not be a valid argument
since there would be other non-parallel items in this
section which should therefore be expunged. Since
there is no textual problem at this point, the only
grounds for deleting the exception clause will be the
interpreter's evaluation of the process of the
transmission of Jesus' teaching. Cf. Myrna and Robert
Kysar, The Asundered (Atlanta: John Knox Press, 1978),
pp. 45-49.

John P. Meier, Law and History in Matthew's
Gospel (Rome: Biblical Institute Press, 1976), pp.
147-59, argues that unchastity (porneia) in 5:32 refers

text will become of greater consequence only if this
section of the Sermon becomes a new study in case-
law. This is not the purpose. The teaching here is
dealing with values or priorities that guide conduct.

        Much has been said above to elaborate and
interpret Jesus' modification of two succinct laws:
"Thou shalt not commit adultery" and "Whoever divorces
his wife . . ." This elaboration has been given to
provide the socio-cultural context in which Jesus
taught. The disciples were aware of the practices of
marriage and divorce of their day as well as the way
the opposite sexes related to each other in general.
The dignity and respect of those relations were as
multi-faceted and multivaried as any society. The
disciples had some sense of the ideal of the proper
relation of the sexes, whether from society in general
or the study of the scriptures specifically. So when
Jesus briefly condemns lustful thoughts and divorce,
the disciples recognize that he is reclaiming the
status of woman to a dignified and worthy partner in
keeping with the intention of the Creator; and by so
doing he has restored the male also to a nobler estate
consistent with the ideal. The intention of Jesus in
the text is not to rewrite casuistry but to call his
disciples to a proper appreciation of the dignity and
worth of human sexuality. The disciple who longs for
God's righteousness--an appropriate relation with God--
will appropriate the Creator's ideal purpose of male
and female as his own value for human sexuality. This
section of the Sermon has now dealt with man's relation
to man and man's relation to the opposite sex. The
next paragraph turns to man's relation to himself.

        The value of integrity beginning with a simple
example of honesty implies a wholeness of personality:

---

to recent converts in the latter church for which
Matthew was written. These converts were already
married in arrangements which violated the laws of
Leviticus 18, thus they were guilty of unchastity and
should divorce. He finds corroborating evidence in
Acts 15:29 and I Cor. 5:1. Joseph A. Fitzmeyer, "The
Matthew Divorce Texts and Some New Palestinian
Evidence," Theological Studies, XXXVII (1976), 197-226,
explores evidence from the Qumran literature on this
point.

Again you have heard that it was said to the men of old, "You shall not swear falsely, but shall perform to the Lord what you have sworn." But I say to you, Do not swear at all, either by heaven, for it is the throne of God, or by the earth, for it is his footstool, or by Jerusalem, for it is the city of the great King. And do not swear by your head, for you cannot make one hair white or black. Let what you say be simply "Yes" or "No"; anything more than this comes from evil.

Mt. 5:33-37

In the usual pattern the text begins with a reference to a prior law, this time about swearing. An exact Old Testament reference cannot be found for v. 33; however, several texts embody the idea:

When a man vows a vow to the Lord, or swears an oath to bind himself by a pledge, he shall not break his word; he shall do all that proceeds out of his mouth.

Num. 30:2

When you make a vow to the Lord your God, you shall not be slack to pay it.

Dt. 23:21

In the Old Testament a "vow" is a promise to give to the Lord something specified on the condition that God granted a favor.[9] Once a person has made the vow or pledge he must carry it out. In a heartrending story in the Old Testament, Jephthah performed what he had sworn (Jg. 11:30-40). The requirement is simple: one must perform what he promises. Although v. 33 does not use the technical word "vow," it does stress the importance of the promise--"what you have sworn"--and the commensurate action--"but shall perform." "Swear falsely" in v. 33 indicates that someone is making an outward promise to perform when there is no inner intention of carrying out the promise. This is a clear recognition that swearing no longer, if ever, was an absolute guarantee of performance. So why should one

---

[9]de Vaux, op. cit., p. 465.

bother with the various gradations of seriousness of oaths, some of which were binding and some were not. The _Mishnah_ contains thirteen pages describing the complex systems of oaths that bound and oaths that did not. Jesus lists only a few--heaven, earth, Jerusalem, and head--and does not bother to elaborate; for it is far more important to simply state one's intention or the truth regarding a matter with a simple "yes" or "no." Anything beyond that "comes from evil."

This paragraph has called to attention two issues: (1) simple truth, the willingness and determination to tell what is right and honest at all times; and (2) the consistency between what one promises and what one performs. Both of these concern the integrity of the individual, the sense of wholeness and harmony that controls his inner disposition. One swears a promise to impress upon others the authenticity of his intention to perform. If he has no intention of performing the promise, he has attempted to deceive his fellowman for his own self aggrandizement; thus he lacks a sense of inner harmony and needs the support of illusory promises. If he makes grandiose promises that he does not have the ability to perform, he is living in a world of fantasy and lacks a sense of inner wholeness that fosters a realistic relation with his fellowman and environment. If one deliberately speaks falsehood, he does so for his own gain or to avoid inconvenience or embarrassment, again, admitting his inability to live with the realities of life.

While Jesus' teaching at this point at first seems ever so simple, it touches on the deepest aspect of human nature. It brings into review how a person relates to his surroundings, how he perceives himself, and what measures he uses to cope with life's situations. It raises the question of how well a person has integrated all of life's experience into a unified inner self which can live in harmony with all facets of his existence. Such a person has developed a consistent lifestyle that is recognized as trustworthy and honest by his fellowman. They can depend on his word because there is an integrity to his total conduct. They have confidence in his conduct because it manifests a pattern of simplicity. He is a man that has set integrity as a value and priority and orders his life accordingly.

The value of self-respect is introduced by the law of _lex talionis_ or a restraint on retaliation. "An eye for an eye and a tooth for a tooth" is a very ancient principal of human civilization. Sometimes the prescribed recovery list continues beyond an eye and tooth:

... hand for hand, foot for foot, burn for burn, wound for wound, stripe for stripe.

Ex. 21:24f.

... fracture for fracture, eye for eye, tooth for tooth, as he has disfigured a man, he shall be disfigured.

Lev. 24:20

Your eye shall not pity; it shall be life for life, eye for eye, tooth for tooth, hand for hand, foot for foot.

Dt. 19:21

Beyond the Old Testament the law code of Hammurabi accepts the same principle and has numerous specific rules elaborating it.[10]

Lex talionis is a valuable principle in human interaction and, when first implemented, represented a major step forward in civilization. Its main function is to restrain retaliation beyond the point of recovering what has been lost or suffered by injury. Man's inclination, stimulated by suffering some wrong, is to respond more forcefully than he has been injured. If tribesmen stole six sheep from a neighboring clan, the inclination would be to recover ten, twelve, or even take the entire herd. If one has a tooth dislodged in a fight, his immediate response might be to injure his opponent more severely. So the law restraining retaliation has a needed function in civilized societies and continues in principle even in modern times.

---

[10]The Code of Hammurabi, 196f., James B. Pritchard, ed. Ancient Near Eastern Texts Relating to the Old Testament (Princeton: University Press, 1969), p. 175.

Societal pressure motivates an individual to seek satisfaction for an injury sustained. It becomes the expected thing and demonstrates one's willingness to be assertive. There are certain rights belonging to everyone, and one of them is the right to recover a loss. When such expectation functions in a group, it becomes important that the individual fulfills the requirement in order to be respected by the group. When this is internalized it becomes a matter of self-respect. Anyone with self-respect will retaliate within the limits of society in an effort to recover his loss or injury. It may even become a matter of honor:

> You have heard that it was said, "An eye for an eye and a tooth for a tooth." But I say to you, Do not resist one who is evil. But if any one strikes you on the right cheek, turn to him the other also; and if any one would sue you and take your coat, let him have your cloak as well; and if any one forces you to go one mile, go with him two miles. Give to him who begs from you, and do not refuse him who would borrow from you.

> Mt. 5:38-42

In this paragraph, Jesus is addressing the matter of self-respect and what criteria the ideal disciple should use in maintaining a sense of self-worth. Jesus modifies the "eye for eye" principle by commanding: "Do not resist one who is evil." The evil one is identified in the four brief examples as the one who injures or makes extreme demands which normally provoke an unkind reaction. The superlative of insults was a slap on the cheek, not because of the pain inflicted, but because it communicated intense denigration from the actor to both the recipient and the witnesses; thus the injured one would feel obligated to respond. But Jesus says "no;" instead, turn the other cheek. By so doing, the ideal disciple would challenge the criteria for self-respect that potentially escalates disharmony, hostility, and hatred. Likewise, in the case of a lawsuit in which the disciple has a definite advantage since he is in possession of his own coat and the burden of proof lies with his opponent, Jesus advises the disciples to quickly give more than is sought even though it will cause significant inconvenience. The cloak was the cape-like garment used for outer wear by day and bedding by night. The point is simple: the disciple will not insist on his traditional rights but rather

will do the unexpected to demonstrate his concern for
rehabilitating inter-human relations.   His concern is
for peace rather than rights.

Peasants in Palestine were often required to
assist a Roman soldier with his baggage for one mile.
This was a degrading drudgery which left the peasant
and soldier greater enemies at the end of the mile.   If
the peasant is willing to forego his anger for the
insult, what potential for peacemaking there would be
as he goes a second mile!   In like manner generosity to
the poor and willingness to lend--an ax, saw, mallet,
or even money--would demonstrate the disciple's concern
for his fellowman.

In each of these examples the disciples are
taught that there are alternate ways to maintain self-
respect other than retaliating or claiming one's
rights.   It is the way of creating peace and harmony
and rehabilitating broken relationships.   This is the
way of the ideal disciple whose commitment is to be a
peacemaker: "Blessed are the peacemakers, for they
shall be called sons of God."

By rejecting the rights provided in an "eye for
eye" principle, Jesus has not rejected man's concern
for self-respect; rather he has reestablished those
things that bring a sense of self-respect.   It is the
life designed out of a concern for the right relation
to God.   The disciple's sense of self-worth will be
determined not by measuring up to societal expectations
but the demand of God.   Jesus has identified the value
of self-respect as an essential priority on which the
disciple will design his life.

The value of love is all encompassing.   It
summarizes the other four values:

You have heard that it was said, "You shall
love your neighbor and hate your enemy." But I say
to you, Love your enemies and pray for those who
persecute you so that you may be sons of your
Father who is in heaven; for he makes his sun rise
on the evil and on the good, and sends rain on the
just and on the unjust. For if you love those who
love you, what reward have you? Do not even the
tax collectors do the same? And if you salute only
your brethren, what more are you doing than
others? Do not even the Gentiles do the same?
You, therefore, must be perfect, as your heavenly
Father is perfect.

                                        Mt. 5:43-48

Jesus' beginning point, "You shall love your neighbor,"
is a quotation from Lev. 19:18, but it is impossible to
find a reference in biblical literature to the last
half of the saying, "and hate your enemy." On the
contrary Lev. 19:34 admonishes the Israelites to
consider the stranger in the land as a native, "and you
shall love him as yourself." It is true that the
Mannual of Discipline (1:4, 10) from The Qumran
Community advises its members to "hate all the sons of
darkness each according to his guilt." The emphasis
there is on the sin of the unfaithful men, and the
saying does not provide the text for Jesus'
comment.[11] From this same era other literature,
however, does give evidence of the vindictive feeling
of the Hebrews towards their Roman overlords. In
referring to the coming Davidic king, a Psalm of
Solomon prays that God will give strength to the king
"that he may shatter unrighteous rulers, and that he
may purge Jerusalem from nations that trample (her)
down to destruction."[12] Another text predicts that
when the "holy prince" comes "there will be inexorable
wrath on Latin men."[13] The bitter conflict that
existed between the Hebrews and Romans in Palestine
could provide a context for the hatred toward enemies
and a cliche suitable to the feeling.[14] At the same
time, first century Hebrew society had numerous
subgroups such as the Sadducees, Pharisees, Essenes,

---

[11]A.R.C. Leaney, The Rule of Qumran and Its
Meaning: Introduction, Translation and Commentary
(London: SCM Press, 1966), pp. 118f., esp. 121.

[12]The Psalms of Solomon 17:24, R. H. Charles,
ed. The Apocrypha and Pseudepigrapha of the Old
Testament (Oxford: At the Clarendon Press, 1913), II,
p. 649. This Psalms was probably written in the first
century before A.D. 70.

[13]The Sibylline Books III, 46-51, Charles, op.
cit., II, p. 379. This selection of the work was
probably written in the first century A.D.

[14]Rodger D. Congdon, "Did Jesus Sustain the Law
in Matthew 5?" Bibliotheca Sacra, CXXXV (April-June,
1978), 125, supports the idea of hatred against the
Romans for the background of this phrase "hate your
enemy."

Herodians, Zealots, etc. They did not always relate in
perfect harmony, and competition and tension between
these groups might also provide a background for the
additional phrase, "hate your enemy," which Jesus has
quoted in order to make his teaching immediately
applicable to his disciples.

Beginning with the position that love and hate
are opposites and that one easily develops an attitude
of hatred towards his enemy, Jesus, in the text,
totally reverses or contradicts the expected. Instead
of a hostile, vindictive, angry feeling toward the
adversary, Jesus insists that the ideal disciple will
love his enemy. He will have the same care and
compassion for his enemy that the older rule idealized
among Israelite neighbors when it commanded, "You shall
love your neighbor." The disciple will extend to his
enemy the same consideration and amenities that he
would offer to an accepted member of his own
community. There will be no discrimination in his
deeds of kindness. The disciple's model for this is
God himself. Sunshine is good. Rain is good. God
gives both to righteous and unrighteous people alike,
even if they are considered enemies by the disciples.
The command to love was to be executed
indiscriminately.

The reader will note that this is the first
occurrence of the word "love" in this Gospel, either
noun or verb. While it was a concept understood by the
hearers of the Sermon, it needed further definition.
What is the attitude of love or what are acts of
love? The command "to love" is immediately defined by
the four preceding paragraphs in which Jesus dealt with
respect for others, the opposite sex, integrity and
truth, and self respect and peacemaking. By
implementing these four values/priorities in his
relation to others the disciple would be carrying out
the command "to love." In other words, the command to
love is the summary paragraph of this section (Mt.
5:17-48), and the previous paragraphs give definition
to the meaning of love.

This final paragraph also introduces a second
new word in the sermon--prayer. The disciple is called
on to "pray for those who persecute you." This
continues the emphasis on the theme of persecution
which was introduced in the beatitudes and further
identified by the "slap on the cheek" and the "forcing
to go a mile," but the present reference adds the note
of prayer. This theme is only introduced here but will

be amplified at least twice before the Sermon is over. Appropriate prayer in this context will motivate the disciple to implement the command.

Moreover, the disciple will be motivated because his devotion to righteousness far exceeds that of the tax collectors and gentiles. This section begins by comparing the righteousness of the disciples with the scribes and Pharisees and is rounded off by the reference just mentioned. On the one hand there is a backward look: be better than those back there; on the other hand there is a forward look: measure up to your heavenly Father. "You, therefore, must be perfect as your heavenly Father is perfect," becomes the final motivation and goal. This is the theme of the beatitudes restated. Righteousness, the appropriate relation with God, is the goal articulated in such phrases as, "They shall see God," and, "They shall be called sons of God." The latter phrase is here repeated as the reward or attainment for the disciple who loves as God loves. He is like God; he is God's son.

Righteousness, the right relation to God, produces in the disciple attitudes and conduct appropriate to that relationship. In fact, the love of God toward all mankind becomes the model for the disciple's attitudes and conduct. The disciple is to measure up to the model--God. This is the meaning of the final verse of the paragraph. Whether the word is translated "perfect," "mature," "complete," or some other synonym the standard is always the same--God. To love one's fellowman in a mature perfect way like God loves is the ultimate desire of the ideal disciple. For him the value of love becomes the summary value that is amplified or defined by the value of human existence, the value of sexuality, the value of integrity, and the value of self-respect.

The same five themes identified in the beatitudes pervade this section which has amplified the beatitudes as it has given definition to righteousness. The ideal disciple is devoted to kingdom righteousness which is the proper relation to God. The proper relation to God in turn produces the ideal disciple whose inner attitudes are controlled by proper values which produce appropriate conduct indiscriminately applied to every person. As the disciple is challenged to consider the values in this section, he is aware of the (1) inner/outer nature of each. Whether it is the value of human existence or

sexuality, there is the inner disposition, even sub-
conscious, which is counterpart to reflexive, outer
patterns of conduct demonstrating one's inner nature.
This inner/outer dimension runs through the other
values as well. One's inner commitment to integrity
and self-respect is the inner part of one's sense of
self-worth which finds subtle expression in myriad
ways. Even love has its inner and outer aspects.

        Likewise (2) the reflection/action theme is
diffused in this section.   One is capable of
reflecting, deliberating, and pondering possible
courses of action both for good or evil at the point of
each value discussed. To pray for one's enemies may
very well lead to kind action toward them. A disciple
about to act on the "second mile" has surely reflected
on what he is about to do, and in time his action may
become reflexive. To contemplate a worthy value will
stimulate appropriate conduct which in turn reinforces
the value contemplated. Through all of this section
the disciple is aware of (3) the heavenly/earthly
tension. He cannot get through to God in heaven if he
is alienated from his fellowman on earth.   If his
thoughts of the opposite sex are unworthy, he should
take drastic action; for it is better to go to heaven
maimed than into hell with all members. Heaven has an
interest in earthly action. Don't swear by heaven.
Become sons of your Father in heaven, but pray on
earth, go the second mile on earth, and turn the other
cheek on earth. The disciple becomes more and more
aware of the imposing influence and demands of the two
realms of heaven and earth.

        Always (4) the God/man relation is evident.
God in heaven expects, even demands, that man on earth
act in such a way that is pleasing to God. The final
verse is clear. Man on earth must be perfect like God
in heaven. God is the model of love which underlies
all other values, and man must measure up to the ideal
which motivates him to the right relation to other
men. (5) The man/man relation is apparent throughout
this section.   All of the values speak to man's
appropriate relation to his fellowman.

        These five themes will permeate the entire
Sermon as the text continues to discuss the ideal
disciple. These themes have not preceded the design of
the Sermon; rather, as the Sermon deals with what God's
righteous kingdom expects of its disciples these themes
become evident as necessary overtones of what is
involved as the ideal disciple follows Jesus in the
kingdom.

The Reader: The Instructed

The reader of this second section of the Sermon
on the Mount feels drawn into the circle of those being
instructed by the author's use of the personal pronoun
"you."   The Sermon is not only addressed to the
disciples on the mountainside in the narrative but also
to any reader of the Gospel. The instructions become
very poignant as the authoritative imperative, "But I
say unto you . . .," is repeated six times in twenty-
eight verses (21-48). The reader begins to sense that
the urgent, unequivocal demands are also intended for
him; and by sensitive reading he will learn much from
this unit.

1.   The reader learns that Jesus, the teacher,
assumes a role of authority with his disciples.   He
boldly assumes the prerogative to modify the long
standing laws by reapplying them to the ideal
disciple. At the beginning of the section, he has made
the acceptance of his teaching the criteria by which
the disciples appropriately relate to the kingdom.
They must not only keep the commandments but teach
others to do so in order to be counted great in the
kingdom (5:19). This reinforces the relation of Jesus
to the kingdom as explained in chapter II, summary 1.

2.   The inner spiritual nature of the ideal
disciple is not directly addressed but will be in
Matthew 6; it is assumed in this section; for the
demand to have proper relations with one's fellowman
presupposes a changed inner disposition.

3.   The reader learns what is meant by "your good
works" (5:16). The series of commands "but I say unto
you" outline the "good works" expected of the disciple.

4.   The reader continues to be reminded of the
possibility of inconvenience and persecution to those
involved with Jesus' teachings.   The beatitudes
identify that persecution will come, and the succeeding
section notes such things as the second mile, law
suits, and praying for those who persecute you.

5.   If the reader concluded the last section of the
Sermon (5:3-16) with a desire to know more about how to
relate to his fellowman, then his desire has been
fulfilled in this section (5:17-48) since the central
concern has been values that control one's life.
Jesus, the teacher, follows a very simple procedure by
beginning with five very familiar laws.   They were

basic to the society of that day and seemed reasonable
enough. Many of his listeners could respond by saying,
"So we have done from our youth." Jesus begins with
the known. He then expands or identifies new frontiers
of application. He modifies and makes new the old
things they know.

Not only is this excellent pedagogy, but it
becomes intellectually profound. For in expanding the
meaning of the simple laws, Jesus has identified four
crucial issues: respect for human existence, respect
for the opposite sex, commitment to integrity, and
proper self-respect. These issues comprehend the
individual's self-understanding as a worthy human being
interacting in a society, however complex. He
understands and appreciates himself and knows how to
relate to his fellowman. All of one's decision-making,
especially moral decisions, are informed and determined
by these four ideas. These are called values; they are
the priorities; they are the guiding principles for
attitudes, decisions, and action. The reader may at
first feel that Jesus is only making another set of
rules since he mentions specific situations in each
paragraph like "whoever calls his brother a fool" or
"give to him who begs." This is not the case. He is
rather using specific illustrations to elucidate the
over-arching principle or value.

The reader should recall two things from the
prior discussion of values. First, values are based on
presuppositions. In the case of Jesus' teaching, the
assumption is that he is the representative of the
heavenly kingdom and thus has authority to teach or
convey appropriate values. In the Gospel of Matthew he
has been identified as the King, Messiah, Immanuel (God
with us), and Son. Furthermore, his teaching is
directed to those who have had a religious experience
as described in the beatitudes (5:3-10). Thus they
have accepted the authoritative position of Jesus. So
the teaching comes from one who has the right to teach
and that right has been accepted by those being
taught. This becomes the presupposition of the values
established.

Secondly, values give rise to rules. This is
inevitable and right. Rules are needed for immediate
situations. They represent the reflective wisdom of a
community seeking to implement the values it holds
dear. Working backwards, one should always be able to
find a value for each rule practiced. Rules become a
burden or seem to be "rules for the sake of rules" when
the relation between the rule and value is no longer
meaningful.

The reader might wish that Jesus had been more specific in each case and applied each value to numerous situations. That would only be disappointing, for already we find that literally going a second mile with a Roman soldier is now totally irrelevant, but to be concerned for what it takes to maintain one's self-respect continues to be an issue. The reader, grasping the profoundness of Jesus' teaching and seeking to implement the values prescribed, may often devise rules growing out of his reflective wisdom to be used as specific aids in developing his own discipleship. The community of disciples, the church, has done this through the ages. Such a process must always be under review lest the rules, losing their direct relation to the values with the passage of time, become "rules for the sake of rules."

The four values have already raised numerous questions in the mind of the reader. How can one love his fellowman and execute him as a criminal or destroy him in war? Does the teaching demand that married partners must remain together even when there is no hope of a loving, happy relationship? Is one permitted to fight back for the sake of survival or to protect others? Is lying to protect others wrong? These and other questions will be addressed in Chapter VI "Actualizing the Ideal."

6. If the reader has read the Sermon carefully, he will notice that the teaching of Jesus has not been set forth as conditions whereby one enters the kingdom, that is by keeping the rules one gains admission. It is assumed throughout the Sermon that the disciples are already believers; they were a part of the kingdom. This is specified in the beatitudes and reiterated in 5:13-16. The teaching of Jesus is presented because the disciples are disciples. "Since you disciples are involved in the kingdom, then here are the values on which you will develop your lives." There is a complete difference in saying, "I am a member because I have implemented the values," and saying, "Since I am a member, I will implement the values." Jesus' teaching is in keeping with the latter. Only disciples who have recognized their dependency upon God and have the appropriate relation with him--righteousness--will hear the teachings of Jesus. Only those who have confirmed their loyalty to Jesus will hear his imperatives.

7. Furthermore, the reader feels the tension created by Jesus' teaching in this section. What ought to be the attitude of the disciple is evident in this

section. The appropriate thought for his fellowman,
the opposite sex, and even his enemies is apparent.
Then the disciple and reader are aware of what is. At
times, Jesus' teaching seems to create a feeling of
guilt rather than a sense of wholeness. The tension
between what one ought to be and what one is becomes
uncomfortable. The solution to this is introduced in
the last paragraph of this section and will be
discussed in the remaining sections of the Sermon.
Jesus admonishes his disciples to "pray for those who
persecute you." The disciples know that they ought to
love their enemies, but they also know how difficult it
is to do such. The clue to doing what ought to be
done, or becoming what one ought to become, is
prayer. The tension created by Jesus' teaching will
continue to grow in the Sermon, and so will his
instruction about prayer.

CHAPTER V

MOTIVATIONAL VALUES

The Sermon on the Mount deals with the ideal relation between man and God. This relation inevitably includes man's relation to his fellowman commensurate with his rightness with God. This has been elaborated in 5:3-48 of the Sermon and specifically emphasized by the word righteousness--"the right conduct of man which follows the will of God and is pleasing to him."[1] So when the fourth sentence of the Sermon blesses those who "hunger and thirst after righteousness" (5:6), the disciple understands that it is a reference to doing God's will. As the Sermon proceeds God's will is associated with the kingdom of heaven and Jesus' own teaching (5:10, 11) for which he claims superiority to others of his day (5:20). Right conduct pleasing to God implies norms. Jesus dealt with the norms or values in 5:21-48 which concluded with the demand for perfection like God. The ultimate norm for right conduct is God himself.

The Instruction: Motivational Values

Now that the "values" have been established, what further instruction to the disciples is appropriate? Earlier in the Sermon, the ideal disciple is encouraged to let his good works be seen of men (5:16). The ill advised disciple might begin to exhibit his discovered values in a blatant manner, so a word of caution is in order:

> Beware of practicing your piety (righteousness) before men in order to be seen by them; for then you will have no reward from your Father who is in heaven.

> Mt. 6:1

Jesus in the Sermon carefully repeated "righteousness" ("piety" in RSV) here so that the disciples would understand that the succeeding paragraphs were essential to a complete understanding of the section on values. Implementing the values in the conduct of a

---

[1]Gottlob Schrenk, TNDT, II, p. 198.

disciple requires not only knowing what is right to do
but also involves the proper motivational values. How
should the disciple be motivated to implement the
ethical values enunciated in 5:20-48. The proper
motivation for ethical conduct is illustrated in three
examples (6:2-18) taken from generally accepted
religious practices of Jesus' day. In fact almsgiving,
prayer, and fasting were the three practices most often
taught by the Pharisees.[2]

Almsgiving, the first example used by Jesus,
was a well established practice based on the laws of
Leviticus 19:9f. and Deuteronomy 24:19-22. The story
of Ruth and Naomi in Boaz's field is a narrative
illustration of this law (Ruth 2). Almsgiving
continued to be of utmost importance throughout the
history of the Hebrew people. It was at times
considered equal to all the commandments of the law and
brought peace between the people and God.[3] An ancient
Hebrew text gives the importance of almsgiving when it,
along with two other considerations is said to be the
condition for rewards in this life as well as in
heaven:

> The following are the things for which a man enjoys
> the fruits in this world while the principal
> remains for him in the world to come: the
> honouring of father and mother, the practice of
> charity, and the making of peace between a man and
> his friend, but the study of the Torah is equal to
> them all.

                                            Peah 1:1[4]

This paragraph along with references to almsgiving
(charity) in the Dead Sea Scrolls accentuates the
concern for the practice among the religious leaders of
the Hebrew people. On one occasion Jesus himself
ordered a would-be disciple to sell all that he owns

---

[2]John Wick Bowman, The Sermon from the Mount
(Philadelphia: Westminster Press, 1957), p. 11.

[3]Benno Przybylski, Righteousness in Matthew and
His World of Thought (Cambridge: Cambridge University
Press, 1980), p. 67.

[4]Quoted from the Babylonian Talmud (London:
Soncino Press, 1948), pt. 5, vol. 32.

and give to the poor. So when Jesus refers to the
practice of almsgiving his disciples are well aware of
its practice:

> "Thus, when you give alms, sound no trumpet before
> you, as the hypocrites do in the synagogues and in
> the streets, that they may be praised by men.
> Truly, I say to you, they have their reward. But
> when you give alms, do not let your left hand know
> what your right hand is doing, so that your alms
> may be in secret; and your Father who sees in
> secret will reward you.

Mt. 6:2-4

The text assumes that the disciples will
practice giving alms. "When," not "if," introduces the
paragraph. The pronoun "you" changes from singular to
plural. The first two occurrences of "you" in verse 2
makes the emphasis on each disciple separately: "When
you, singularly, do alms . . ." The plural comes out
in the phrase "truly, I say to you . . .," but returns
to the singular form in verse 3 for the remainder of
the paragraph. This change from singular to plural is
demonstrated in the text above where the singular forms
are underscored.[5]   The change is a grammatical
technique designed to entice the listener/reader to be
involved in the text of the Sermon.

The pedagogical method in this paragraph is
very simple: the contrast between the wrong and the
right way to give alms. The wrong way is pictured as
an ostentatious display of one's almsgiving activity in
such a way as to maximize public attention to the
giver. The person described in the wrong way to give
alms is concerned solely for the attention he gets in
the process. This could be called "giver centered"
charity. His reward is being noticed. The phrase
"they have" is the word used in everyday commercial
activities to confirm that a debt or bill has been
"paid in full." So when seen by others, the "giver
centered" person has been fully paid for his trouble.
He got what he wanted.

The right way to give alms is in contrast with
this, for the giver avoids all public display of his
activity and does not even let his closest associates
know what he is doing: the left hand doesn't know what
the right hand is doing. This cloak of secrecy about
the whole matter assures the almsgiver that his reward
is from God.

In these two contrasts Jesus asserts that simply practicing what seems to be good conduct is not necessarily righteousness before God. While righteous deeds are an integral part of the ideal disciples' participation in the kingdom of heaven, the motivation of the deed is important too. Throughout his teaching in the ethical section, Jesus continually maintained the emphasis on the inner disposition of the disciple. This emphasis is present in this paragraph also. The disciple does not practice his righteous conduct in order to be lauded by men. Those who have little interest in Jesus' teaching could do that. The true disciple is motivated at a deeper level. He simply wishes to please God, and by avoiding public exhibit of his action he has the satisfaction of knowing his motivation is appropriate.

This paragraph follows closely the paragraph in which Jesus describes God's good deeds toward the just and unjust and admonishes the disciples to be like-minded so that so that they may be sons of God (5:45). Something of the former motivation is carried over to this paragraph. The disciple does what is appropriate because it is the will of God. He does not seek outward credit; he wishes only to act out the ideal of "Blessed are the merciful;" so he accepts the privilege of almsgiving without any thought of applause.

The question may be asked if Jesus chose the example of almsgiving only because it was a cherished practice of his day or were there other reasons. Almsgiving is an essential institution so long as there are poor and needy in the land. Without it they could not survive. Alms actually maintained the existence of those in need. Jesus, earlier in the Sermon, has taught his disciples to have absolute respect for human existence; they are not to destroy or degrade their fellowman. Almsgiving speaks to the positive side. The disciples are to practice alms in order to maintain life. The disciples are motivated to give alms because of their deep regard for human life and because it is pleasing to God.

The disciples would not overlook the fact that Jesus mentions a reward. As they are properly motivated in their righteous deeds, God will reward them. In this paragraph the reward is not specified; however, the disciples must recall that Jesus began the Sermon with a description of the ideal disciple which description included both conditions and rewards. The reward in the beginning poem was the kingdom of heaven and all its benefits. The practice of almsgiving is used to further amplify the seed ideas in the opening section, so also the rewards mentioned here will take their substance from the opening paragraph.[6]

In this example of almsgiving Jesus has not discussed specific needs, times, places, or described the recipients. He has given a succinct general example that contrasts the right with the wrong. The point is to teach proper motivation for any situation. The disciple strives to implement the teaching of Jesus as the expression of the will of God. He is motivated simply because it is God's will. He is motivated because he is implementing the ethical ideals of Jesus, and that is precisely the point of this section of the Sermon. "Be careful the way you put into practice your righteousness." So the example of almsgiving is not isolated, rather it illustrates the appropriate motivation for all of the disciple's conduct as he implements the teaching of Jesus.

Prayer, like almsgiving, was a normal practice of Jesus' day. Prayers were said in unison in the Temple in Jerusalem and in the synagogue ceremonies throughout Palestine and wherever synagogues were located in the larger Roman world. The Psalms, both within sacred scripture as well as those recorded elsewhere, are evidence of the presence of appropriate prayers among the people. Although there were formal fixed prayers, such as the Eighteen Benedictions, the pious worshiper could offer his own personal prayer. Fixed times of prayer were established for weekdays; and one could stop wherever he might be, assume a posture of prayer, and with moving lips whisper a prayer. Such a system of prayer could easily be misused by those who sought religious security by conforming to the letter of the law. Their motivation to pray could be questioned. Jesus' instruction to his disciples avoids this:

And when you pray, you must not be like the hypocrites; for they love to stand and pray in the synagogues and at the street corners, that they may be seen by men. Truly, I say to you, they have their reward. But when you pray, go into your room

---

[6]Cf. pp. 26f.

and shut the door and pray to your Father who is in
secret; and your Father who sees in secret will
reward you.

Mt. 6:5-6

Again, the form is that of contrast between the
right way and the wrong way. There were those who made
a vain display of their prayer life taking every
opportunity to be seen of men. That seems to be what
motivated them. When they did this, the text asserts
that they have been paid in full--"received their
reward." Unfortunately they missed the purpose and
benefits of prayer.

Prayer was accepted as a worthy religious
activity and the disciples would certainly practice
it. They must be instructed properly. When Jesus
begins his directions to his disciples the text changes
from "you" plural in verse 5 to "you" singular in verse
6. This is illustrated by the underscored words in the
above text. This change is an effort to individualize
the instruction for emphasis. So the directions are
for you, alone, to go into your room, close your door,
and pray. The room designated was a small storage room
attached to the house and probably the only room having
a door.[7] It was not built for use by the members of
the family. Thus there would be isolation from the
traffic of the household. The disciple would be free
to communicate with God without the demand to perform
in the presence of others. His true feelings and needs
could be opened to God without embarrassment. The
disciple could begin to enjoy the purpose and benefits
of prayer: communication with God in such a way as to
remove any barriers to full accord and reestablish an
intimate relation between the disciple and God. This
will include forgiveness and concern for the needs of
the disciple. This is the reward which God will bring
to the petitioner. Again it is the same reward that
Jesus has offered in the opening poem and identified in
the above section of almsgiving. The reward for a
correct prayer life is the kingdom and its benefits.

The disciples must be careful the way they
practice their righteousness, their conduct that is
pleasing to God. An assessment of their prayer life

---

[7]Eduard Schweizer, The Good News According to
Matthew (Atlanta: John Knox Press, 1975), p. 145.

will be a good indicator of their motivation. Like almsgiving, prayer must be motivated by a concern for the inner life of the disciple and his relation to God rather than an effort to impress others with his piety. Prayer must be God centered self-concern rather than audience centered self-interest.

Jesus' instructions on prayer would have been symmetrical with the paragraphs on almsgiving and fasting if the text had stopped at this point. Instead the subject of prayer is continued to include a second contrast, with the gentiles, and an example of a worthy prayer.

The contrast of the hypocrites' prayer with the disciples' proper prayers reorients the prayer to God rather than a display before man. The contrast with the gentiles' prayers brings into focus the content of prayer:

> And in praying do not heap up empty phrases as the Gentiles do; for they think that they will be heard for their many words. Do not be like them, for your Father knows what you need before you ask him.

> Mt. 6:7-8

The non-Hebrew religions of the ancient world honoured their deities with prayer and petitions. Verse 7 alludes to the practices of repetitious words and phrases in such prayers. This was done by reciting a long list of honorific words in front of the deity's name in an effort to insure that the god would hear and respond because he had been flattered by such gracious words.[8] In contrast to this practice Jesus assures the disciples that God's sensitivity to their needs is not dependent on their lengthy sentences. In fact God knows their needs before they speak. Jesus was aware of God's promise of old:[9]

> Before they call I will answer
> While they are yet speaking I will hear

> Is. 65:24

---

[8]The prayers of the priests of Baal in 1 Kg. 18:26-29 is a good example of this.

[9]This reference is from Schweizer, op cit., p. 147.

Thus Jesus removes from the concern of the disciples
any formula of address necessary to insure a successful
prayer and refocuses the substance of prayer on what
God can do for the one genuinely praying. The true
motive in prayer is not how beautifully the disciple
addresses God but rather how open he is to God. The
motivation for prayer is borne out of a need to hear
God rather than to tell God. This is a benefit of the
disciple's seeking the kingdom type righteousness from
a pure motive:

> Our Father who art in heaven,
> Hallowed be thy name.
> Thy kingdom come,
> Thy will be done,
>   on earth as it is in heaven.
> Give us this day our daily bread,
> And forgive us our debts,
>   As we also have forgiven our debtors;
> And lead us not into temptation,
>   But deliver us from evil.

Mt. 6:9-13

The first word in the English text "our"
signals that Jesus takes the point of view of the
disciples as he instructs them in the matter of
prayer. This grammatical change from the second to the
first person is normal in the situation and permits the
prayer to be taught in a more realistic and intimate
manner. So the disciples are taught to approach God in
their prayers by the address "our Father who art in
heaven."

"Our Father" has been deliberately chosen to
impress upon the disciples as they pray the nearness of
God and the intimate relation they have with him. The
idea of God as "Father" is not new in Jesus'
teaching. Its use can be illustrated from the Hebrew
scriptures[10] as well as the sacred literature of the
ancient Near East. The new dimension that Jesus brings
to the title "Father" is the change from the formal
word for father in the Aramaic language to the use of
an everyday word, a homey "family word." Behind Jesus'
use of the English "father" lies the Aramaic word <u>Abba</u>
which appears in the New Testament in Mk. 14:63, Rom.

---

[10]Dt. 32:6; Mal. 2:10; Ps. 103:13f.; Ex. 4:22;
Jer. 3:4f., 19f.; et al.

8:15, and Gal. 4:6. Abba was never before used by
pious Hebrews as an address to God. This change in the
word for father in addressing God is a major
characteristic of Jesus' teaching. God, the heavenly
Father is near and dear to the disciples whom Jesus is
teaching.[11]

        For the disciples to overcome his reverent awe
for the heavenly deity and address him as "our Father"
was   a   major   breakthrough   in   their   religious
pilgrimage. Jesus has carefully prepared them for this
experience in the Sermon. When he refers to God in the
opening poem, which is a generalization of the ideal
disciple, Jesus refers to God with the simple word
"God" (5:8,9). While the term "God" appears three more
times in the Sermon (5:34; 6:24, 30), the context is
somewhat impersonal; for at the same time the text of
the Sermon shifts grammatically from the third person
to the second person it begins to use the term "your
Father."   The disciples could not miss the point:
Jesus is asserting that God in heaven may be addressed
by them in an intimate fashion. By the time Jesus
presents the prayer beginning "our Father," he has used
the phrase "your Father" eight times for the
disciples.[12]   Following the prayer the term "your
Father" is again used eight times. It seems almost by
design that "our Father" stands midpoint in the Sermon
in relation to the use of "Father" as a reference to
God; however, the Sermon is certainly designed to teach
the disciples that God's presence is a reality for
them; and the prayer beginning "our Father" confirms
this.

        "The one in the heavens" is added to "our
Father" to avoid closeness that leads to
manipulation. "In the heavens" is describing "God's
world in its infinite difference from that of
mankind."[13]   God's distance from mankind and his

---

[11]For the information in this paragraph I am
indebted to Joachim Jeremias, The Prayers of Jesus
(London: SCM Press, 1967), esp. pp. 96f.; and Ernst
Lohmeyer, "Our Father" (New York: Harper & Row, 1965),
esp. ch. 2.

[12]Plural "you" 5:16; 5:45; 5:48; 6:1,8;
singular "you" 6:4, 6 bis.

[13]Lohmeyer, op. cit., p. 34.

difference, otherness, is further underscored by the
petition: "Hallowed be thy name." "Your name is to be
holy." God's holiness, otherness, was a basic idea of
the Hebrew religion. In Leviticus 19:1 God declares,
"I the Lord your God am holy." Following in this
tradition the prayer asks that God be recognized as the
holy other one whose infinite domain is beyond all
human conception, yet so intimately close to the
disciples he may be addressed as "our Father." This is
the reward for the ideal disciple who received Jesus'
instruction.

As the prayer continues, the disciples
earnestly desire that God's heavenly realm will break
into the earthly abode of man and that his holy will
will be as active on earth as it is in heaven. "Thy
kingdom come . . . will be done . . ." The reflective
disciple will be able to put together this petition
with the prior teaching of Jesus in the Sermon. The
picture of the ideal disciple, the ethical values, and
proper motivation are all a part of God's will. The
disciple is to be like God (5:48) and seek to please
him (6:4,6). The scope of God's will is all inclusive,
yet a part of his will is specifically known to the
disciples, and their prayer is that it will begin to
take effect in them here on earth.

Verses 9 and 10 are an expression of the
disciples' concern for their relation to God. Verse 11
turns to a proper concern for the things of life. It,
however, simply asks for a portion of bread (food) that
will sustain them for one day. Such a prayer brings to
the surface the matter of dependency. The disciples,
recognizing their absolute dependence upon God, do not
ask for rations to last a life time, but only enough
for the immediate need. Jesus, in teaching this
petition, recognizes the need for sustenance as well as
the problems of misplaced security when one has an over
abundance.[14]

Verse 12 identifies the need for forgiveness
and reconciliation between "our Father" and the
disciples and also between the disciple and his
fellowman. This verse prays that Jesus' previous
instruction on hatred will indeed be implemented in
their lives.

---

[14]The story of the rich fool in Lu. 12:13-21 is
a narrative illustrating this point.

Verse 13 is concerned for the problem of temptation and evil, and the two parts of the sentence should be taken together to mean, not testing, but deliverance. Jesus is teaching the disciple to recognize the serious potential of testing by the struggle between the kingdom of heaven and forces of evil. The struggle was not put to an end, and their human resources were not strong enough to overcome it. Only by their absolute dependence upon God's deliverance could they overcome. In the opening verses of the Sermon Jesus warns the disciples of testing through persecution (5:10,11). So the prayer gives assurance to those tested.[15] The closing sentence appearing in the KJV is not in the oldest manuscripts. It was probably modeled after I Chron. 29:11-13, and was used by the early Christians to conclude the prayer when they used it in worship. Verses 14 and 15 are an amplification of verse 12.

<u>Fasting</u> is a natural extension of prayer. Prayer is communicating, listening, receiving. Fasting, in its ideal expression, is a deliberate exercise to facilitate and bring about a desired spiritual condition. Fasting ideally and otherwise was practiced by religious people of Jesus' day. Jesus uses the same paragraph structure to discuss fasting that he has used in discussing almsgiving and prayer. The conclusion is that the disciples must use fasting for what it will do for them rather than the credit it will bring from their fellowman. The paragraph on fasting further amplifies the admonition to be careful how they practice their righteousness. Right conduct before God comes from a properly motivated heart.

This unit of the Sermon begun in 6:1 with the subject of practicing righteousness is completed with the summary reference to righteousness in 6:33; however, there is a sub-division of the unit at the end of verse 18 when the three concrete examples of right conduct have been completed and the thought turns toward less concrete activities.

---

[15]If the reader is concerned for the problem of God's leading disciples into temptation, it is not appropriate to think that God tempts, rather God permits one to be tempted by evil, yet dependency upon him is the source of overcoming.

These first 18 verses of chapter 6 have to do with proper motivation. What values or priorities motivate the disciple to righteousness? The three examples of almsgiving, prayer, and fasting are given first of all to demonstrate the proper motivation. Why should one act righteous? The illustrations make it clear that the disciples' actions are motivated out of a desire to please God. The discussion of these three examples grows out of the prior teaching in the Sermon. The disciples are taught to hunger and thirst for righteousness, and Jesus' ethical ideals provide the substance for the righteousness, and God provides the model (5:48). Then the desire to please God will motivate the disciple to appropriate action. True motivation is met with the reward of knowing that the disciple is a part of the kingdom and its blessing.

So almsgiving, prayer, and fasting are illustrations that the primary motivational value in implementing Jesus' teaching is simply to please God. At the same time the practice of the three exercises have meaning within themselves. Almsgiving extends the respect for human existence; fasting expresses the disciples' sincere desire to bring about the desired spiritual disposition in his life; and prayer is opening oneself to God.

Of the three, prayer is the most important because more space has been devoted to it. The model prayer becomes the central matter of this section and significantly stands at the center of the entire Sermon. The motivation to righteous conduct pleasing to God as outlined by Jesus and all the blessings and benefits of the kingdom as offered by Jesus are brought together when Jesus teaches his disciples to address God by the phrase "our Father in the heavens." In this address, the deity who is far away, remote, cloaked in awful holiness, beyond the world of the disciples, is brought as close to them as a loving, caring, compassionate, homey father. In this single phrase Jesus has brought his disciples a simple understanding of the kingdom of heaven: God's presence is real to motivate disciples to act appropriately to his kingdom. The disciples need only to open themselves, to pray, and the blessing will be theirs. This is why a disproportionate amount of space was given to the subject of prayer.

At the same time the prayer is the disciple's confirmation that he recognizes his dependency upon God for his spiritual existence as well as his physical

needs, that he has begun to implement the heavenly
values in his own life, and that his escape from evil
is possible only by the help of God. The theme of the
prayer may be summarized as the disciple's affirmation
of dependency upon God. This is the beginning point of
the disciple's ability to implement the demands of the
Sermon.

        In this section (6:18) the five contrasting
themes observed in the other sections are found. (1)
The inner/outer is present throughout the three
illustrations as the proper inner motivation is
contrasted with the improper outer desire for
approval. The disciple is challenged (2) to "reflect"
upon his spiritual condition through prayer and fasting
as he "acts" consistent with the will of God. (3) The
heavenly/earthly contrast is obvious in the model
prayer when the disciple on earth prays to "our Father
in the heavens." Also the constant reference to "your
Father who sees" reminds the disciples that (4) the
God/man relation is found throughout the section, not
only in the model prayer but the effort of man to
please God. (5) The unwholesome aspect of the man/man
relation is highlighted by those who practice their
religious activities to be applauded by others while
the positive relation is expressed in the prayer for
forgiveness and amplified in vv. 14-15.   These
contrasting themes represent the dynamic relations that
influence the life of the disciple.

                The Reader: The Instructed

        In the previous chapter three levels of
discussing right and wrong were identified: (1) What
are the rules? (2) What are the values? (3) Why be
moral?   Chapter three dealt with question (2).
Question (3) Why be moral? underlies the present
chapter in a modified form: What values motivate one
to practice the moral precepts known to him?   What
priorities encourage one to live consistent with a
system of guidelines?

        1.   The reader of the Sermon has already
learned that ideal disciples (5:3-16) are presented
with a set of values (5:17-48) worthy of implementation
because Jesus has claimed the authority to teach
them.   At the end of the discussion (5:48) "your
heavenly Father" becomes the model of implementing the
values. This leaves a bit of uneasiness in the mind of
the disciple/reader, for who can be like God? Who can
function with the lofty values given?

2. Jesus assumes the disciple can and proceeds to offer instruction for implementing the righteousness he has just enunciated. The reader quickly learns that the disciple's conduct must be designed to please God. As this becomes the basic motivation the outward conduct of almsgiving, prayer, and fasting will be appropriate. Furthermore, this same motivation can be applied to the five values in 5:17-48: human existence, sexuality, integrity, self-respect, and love. The reader begins to put together the ideas in the Sermon. All of the values are to be implemented to please God rather than others; but in so doing others will be served. While the emphasis is on the inner disposition and motivation of the disciple, the welfare of his fellowman is not ignored. One serves his fellowman best when properly motivated.

3. The reader discovers a new dimension in this section--the concept of reward. This was mentioned in 5:45 with a reference to the disciples becoming sons of "your Father who is heaven." The promise of God's reward is repeated in each paragraph and is specifically identified by Jesus when he teaches the disciples to address God as "our Father."

4. The ability to know God as "our Father" becomes the ultimate motivational priority. If this relation has been established through the dependency of the disciple upon God as amplified in the model prayer, then the demands of the Sermon's values, however difficult, will begin to fall into place.

5. The reader, whether on the first reading of the Sermon or on a later critical reading, must grasp the fact that "our Father in the heavens" is the central point of the Sermon. What has been taught before in the Sermon comes into clear focus in light of this concept, and what succeeds this point in the Sermon takes its reference for it.

6. The nature of prayer comes to the surface in this section. While prayer includes petition, its essential characteristic is the recognition of dependency upon God and an openness to receive from God.

7. In this section the inner life of the disciple begins to have contours. He is a man of prayer, devotion, and compassion for his fellowman.

Beginning in 6:19 the disciple's devotion to his heavenly Father is amplified.

CHAPTER VI

THE ULTIMATE VALUE

The ethical values set forth by Jesus in Mt. 5 is the substance of righteous behavior pleasing to God. It is summarized in 5:48 with the admonition to be perfect as "your heavenly Father." Chapter 6 of Matthew continues the Sermon by elaborating the appropriate way to practice this righteousness. The use of the word righteousness (5:6,10,20; 6:1,33) and the use of "your heavenly Father" (5:16,45,48; 6:1,4,6,8,9,14,15,18,26,32) maintain the continuity of thought between chapters 5 and 6. Chapter 6 is marked out as a unit at the beginning and end by a reference to "righteousness": "Beware of practicing your piety [righteousness]" (6:1); "But seek first his kingdom and his righteousness" (6:33). The entire chapter has to do with motivation to seek "his righteousness." There is a slight change in structure beginning in 6:19 as the text moves beyond the three specific activities of almsgiving, prayer, and fasting to a more general discussion of the ultimate value of absolute devotion to God.

The Instruction

Matthew 6:19-34 emphasizes different aspects of the ultimate value by four paragraphs using different imagery. Each paragraph is centered around some simple, obvious situation in life that is easily understood and needs no explanation or debate. With a few terse words the situation is applied to the importance of recognizing the ultimate value.

Do not lay up for yourselves treasures on earth, where moth and rust consume and where thieves break in and steal, but lay up for yourselves treasures in heaven, where neither moth nor rust[1] consumes and where thieves do not break in and steal. For where your treasure is, there will your heart be also.

Mt. 6:19-21

---

[1]The Greek word translated "rust" may also refer to "rot" which eats away a fragile box.

Treasure is used by Jesus in the text as a literary image for the outward expression of a disciple's inner devotion. The parable-like story is easily comprehended. If a disciple works diligently to accumulate a treasure, it is because he is motivated by a scheme, plan, goal, or life-long ambition. Something in his inner being guides his conduct in collecting the treasure to the end that it may be said his heart is in his treasure. The Sermon has earlier (5:18) used the concept of "heart" to identify that aspect of the human personality that thinks, deliberates, and controls conduct. Jesus here makes, for the disciples, a direct connection between one's outward designed actions and one's inner thinking. The disciple must therefore be careful that his outward activities are consistent with his inner commitment lest his sincere devotion is diluted.

The disciple must be concerned for his treasure in heaven. By making this reference to heaven continuity is maintained with the preceding paragraph which mentions "your Father . . . in secret;" and the idea of treasure meshes with the rewards from the Father. This is an effort to maintain the flow of compatible imagery in the Sermon. Further continuity is maintained by the pedagogical method of contrasts. There are two places to accumulate treasure: in heaven or on earth.

The brief comparison of the two depositories for treasure make it obvious which is of greater worth, so the disciple listening cannot miss the point. He must choose the higher priority of heaven, and in so doing both his outward conduct and his inner decision-making ability (heart) will be controlled thereby.

The eye is the lamp of the body. So if your eye is sound, your whole body will be full of light; but if your eye is not sound, your whole body will be full of darkness. If then the light in you is darkness, how great is the darkness!

Mt. 6:22-23

The eye transmits a sense of reality to the individual. This vital sensory receptor was perceived in Jesus' day to bring light to the body in contrast to darkness which engulfed the blind person. Although the disciples were not aware of modern theories of eye diseases and disorders, they, like Jesus, knew that some people had only partial vision which brought a

distorted sense of reality. In one story from Jesus'
healing ministry a man reports that he sees "men; but
they look like trees" (Mk. 8:24). If the eye transmits
false or distorted signals to the person, he will
develop his entire behavioral response to an erroneous
sense of reality. This would be a disastrous
situation. Therefore, it is absolutely essential to
have a valid sense of reality. Jesus does not have to
make an explicit application for his disciples. The
lesson is obvious. If they fashion their lives on a
false sense of reality, i.e. a false premise, then
their entire life will be in error. How dreadful!

     This simple description of the eye reinforces
the point of being devoted to the proper treasure as
well as being concerned for the reward from "your
Father." It forces the disciple to examine the basic,
singular premise upon which they will design their
existence. Whatever the commitment it will control and
integrate their life. The focus of this point is
sharpened in the next paragraph.

     No one can serve [be a slave to] two masters;
     for either he will hate the one and love the other,
     or he will be devoted to the one and despise the
     other. You cannot serve God and mammon.

                                        Mt. 6:24

     The slave was totally under the control of his
owner. He may be well educated or a master
craftsman. Captives of war often became slaves, and
there were no racial overtones associated with the
practice.[2] The declaration that no slave can serve two
masters is undebatable since two bosses cannot have
total claim on one worker. The disciples would agree
with their teacher. The two masters contrast is then
applied to God and mammon. The disciples would
immediately associate God with "our Father" and clearly
knew the meaning of "mammon." This word has been
brought, untranslated, from Aramaic to Greek to
English. The word itself has a neutral connotation and
simply refers to "property" as a reference from the
Mishnah will attest:

     [2]W.F. Albright and C. S. Mann, Matthew (New
York: Doubleday & Company, Inc., 1971), p. 81.

R. Jose said: Let the property of thy fellow be dear to these as thine own; and fit thyself for the study of the Law, for [the knowledge of] it is not thine by inheritance; and let all thy deeds be done for the sake of Heaven.

Aboth 2:12[3]

"Mammon" is used in Luke 6:9ff. where it is qualified by the word "unrighteous" leaving the impression that without the qualifying word "mammon" is neutral.

For the disciples to hear the word as a neutral reference to all property imposes a stricter teaching than if "mammon" is a reference to property obtained by evil, deceitful, measures.[4] The conclusion of the saying is precise. "You, my disciples, cannot be a slave to two bosses, it is absolutely impossible." The disciple's loyalty is unequivocally stated: he must be totally loyal to the ultimate value of absolute devotion to God.

If the three short paragraphs of instructions about treasures, eye, and slave have lacked specific application, the next paragraph will bring the need for application as well as further definition of "mammon."

Therefore I tell you, do not be anxious about your life, what you shall eat or what you shall drink, nor about your body, what you shall put on. Is not life more than food, and the body more than clothing? Look at the birds of the air: they neither sow nor reap nor gather into barns, and yet your heavenly Father feeds them. Are you not of more value than they? And which of you by being anxious can add one cubit to his span of life? And why be anxious about clothing? Consider the lilies of the field, how they grow; they neither toil nor spin, yet I tell you even Solomon in all his glory was not arrayed like one of these. But if God so

---

[3]Translation from The Mishnah, trans. Herbert Danby (Oxford: University Press, 1933), p. 449.

[4]Eduard Schweizer, The Good News According to Matthew (Atlanta: John Knox Press, 1975), p. 164. In my judgment the emphasis on the derogatory use of "mammon" is overdone by F. Hauck, TDNT, IV, p. 388f.

clothes the grass of the field, which today is
alive and tomorrow is thrown into the oven, will he
not much more clothe you, O men of little faith?
Therefore do not be anxious saying, "What shall we
eat?" or "What shall we drink?" or "What shall we
wear?" For the Gentiles seek all these things; and
your heavenly Father knows that you need them
all. But seek first his kingdom and his
righteousness, and all these things shall be yours
as well.

Therefore do not be anxious about tomorrow, for
tomorrow will be anxious for itself. Let the day's
own trouble be sufficient for the day.

Mt. 6:25-34

Seek first his kingdom is the theme of the
final paragraph which opens with an emphatic "Because
of this I am saying to you . . ." The disciples would
reintensify their attention at such a statement and be
attentive to what was about to be said because it will
be a fuller explanation of what they have just heard.
"Therefore" or "Because of this" follows immediately
the word "mammon" indicating a connection to the
sentence just concluded. Because it is totally
impossible to serve God and mammon, Jesus will explain
further.

The disciples will note that their teacher
returns to the intimate use of "your heavenly Father"
which has been in the background since verse 18. He is
the one who feeds the birds (v. 26) and knows the needs
of the disciples (v. 32), and it is his kingdom and its
righteousness which the disciples must seek first.
This extends the reference to God in the God/mammon
contrast in v. 25.

The mammon side of the contrast is amplified by
those things about which the disciples will have
anxiety, and surely they will since Jesus has just
asserted that they cannot be in with God, "our Father,"
if they are motivated by mammon. Such a statement
would produce immediate anxiety. Since Jesus knew
this, he immediately says, "Don't be anxious," and
proceeds to list those things which cause anxiety:
food, drink, and clothing. These are the very things
that mammon provides for the disciples. Without these
things they cannot survive. Jesus knew the necessities
of human life, and he was sensitive to the disciples'
desire for a worthy commitment to "our Father." His
statement to them is not that they must ignore the

sustenance of life but rather that they put it in proper perspective with the kingdom of heaven and not be unduly concerned. So Jesus gives the disciples several reasons why they should not be anxious about the things that mammon supplies. First, there is more to a human being than food and clothing; food and clothing is not enough; one must have the kingdom first. Second, the heavenly Father cares for the things in nature: birds, lilies, grass. The disciples are more important. Even if they are overly concerned, will it really add to the length of life?

The disciples would be aware that Jesus repeats the word "anxious" six times in this closing paragraph. Either the prior teaching has created anxiety or Jesus was anticipating the disciples' anxiety and striving to fortify them against it. The former is the reason, for the sharp contrast between being a slave to God or mammon was extremely threatening to Palestinian men, some of whom still owned commercial fishing gear on the Sea of Galilee.

While the thought of this paragraph expands mammon to include the things that sustain life, it also expands the role of the heavenly Father who provides for his children: "Your heavenly Father knows that you need them all." This echoes the introduction to the model prayer: "Your Father knows what you need before you ask him" (6:8). In fact, the anxiety created by the tension between mammon and God is anticipated in the model prayer; and the line, "give us this day our daily bread," is the disciples' declaration of dependency upon the Father for the things that sustain life. The disciples should begin to note that the Sermon builds upon itself to reinforce itself as it proceeds from paragraph to paragraph.

This final paragraph as well as the three short preceding paragraphs emphasize the same theme: The ultimate value is absolute devotion to God. This theme grows out of being careful to practice righteousness in order to please God. The stringent demands of this section leave no place for ambiguity of commitment and loyalty to the kingdom. Such demands may produce anxiety in the disciple if he interprets Jesus' word to mean that a disciple can forget the menial activities that sustain life. "Do not be anxious" does not equal "forget about it." It means place in the proper perspective. Do not be controlled by the things that sustain life. The controlling force in the disciple will not be concern for the things of life but rather the kingdom of heaven.

But seek ye first his kingdom
and his righteousness and
all these things will be yours as well.

v. 33

When the disciples accept the kingdom and righteousness
of "our Father" in heaven as the ultimate value, then
mammon, the things that sustain life, and all else will
fit into place, even the appropriate concern for
tomorrow (v. 34).

The underlying themes of the Sermon continue in
this section. The most prominent are the
heavenly/earthly and the God/man themes. Man on earth
must relate to God in heaven with ultimate devotion.
The two spheres and the two parties are interrelated.
Heaven thrusts its presence into the earthly abode of
man and requires a response. This section in general
is turned inward and involves the reflective nature of
man. While outward activity may be implied, it is not
the basic concern here. Man, inwardly, must feel the
claims of heaven and decide what his commitment will
be.

The Reader: The Instructed

In Matthew 6 the reader has been led through
the section that begins and ends with an emphasis on
righteousness. This concept developed through the
Sermon refers to the disciples' right relationship with
God, which relationship leads to conduct pleasing to
God. Mt. 6:1-18 described the appropriate motivation
for right conduct, and 6:19-34 makes plain that such
motivation is possible only when the ultimate value is
properly identified and accepted.

Values refer to those priorities or important
principles which a person uses to make decisions about
his life and conduct. Most human beings have a system
or group of values that guide their lives. To speak of
ultimate value is to refer to that one single interest
point, priority, or personal commitment which controls
all other sub-values in a person's life. Matthew 6:19-
34 is concerned for the ultimate value.

1. The reader learns that Jesus taught the
disciples the importance of recognizing that they have
values, priorities, and goals which direct the course
of their conduct and life. Their inner commitment,

however hazily formulated, worked together with their outward acts to accomplish their goals.

2. Since the inner commitment is so important, the disciples must be sure it is the correct one. This is the zero point, the point of departure, the direction giving signal; therefore, the disciples must be sure they have the right one.

3. The reader along with the disciples become anxious at the absolute demand of Jesus that forces a choice between God and earthly property--mammon--which supplies the needs for human survival. The demand is precise. God is the ultimate value.

4. The reader learns along with the disciple that there is a way to cope with the anxiety created: absolute trust and dependency upon the heavenly Father. When the ultimate priority is accepted, the sub-values will find their proper place.

5. The reader detects that anxiety at this point was very real for the disciples, and by the end of chapter 6 he has developed a genuine sympathy for the disciples who are receiving the instruction. The instruction has gradually built to an impossible demand, at least an abandonment of the normal patterns of human existence. The beatitudes ended with a blessing to those who are persecuted for righteousness, and the disciples' righteousness must exceed that of others. The righteousness demanded of the disciples is set forth in the series of modified precepts that appear to be unattainable, ending in the ultimate demand to be like God. They are further instructed in the appropriate way to practice their religious activities along with a requirement of priorities that also appear to be unattainable.

CHAPTER VII

ACTUALIZING THE IDEAL

The Sermon now turns to provide the disciples directions and support whereby they may begin to actualize the ideals presented to them. An author or speaker must offer some clue to the accomplishment of his instruction or his ideal will be no more than an implausible fantasy. The last unit of the Sermon (7:1-27) explains how the disciples can appropriate the teaching. It begins by continuing the grammatical use of the second person imperative: "Judge not." This maintains the intimate relation between Jesus and his disciples, but before the section is complete there is a deliberate shift to the third person. This section is composed of seven paragraphs which are not always parallel in form, but in each of them there is a contrast which is characteristic of the pedagogical method in the Sermon.

The Instruction

Judge not, that you be not judged. For with the judgment you pronounce you will be judged, and the measure you give will be the measure you get. Why do you see the speck that is in your brother's eye, but do not notice the log that is in your own eye? Or how can you say to your brother, "Let me take the speck out of your eye," when there is the log in your own eye? You hypocrite, first take the log out of your own eye, and then you will see clearly to take the speck out of your brother's eye.

Mt. 7:1-5

The little story is in the form of an hyperbole. The disciples smiled when they imagined a physician working desperately to remove a speck from a patient's eye never noticing the log in his own eye. How ridiculous! After the original smile, they realized that Jesus was directing the story towards them; for throughout the paragraph the same "you" continues that has been found in the Sermon: "You, my disciples." The smile soon changed into serious concern when Jesus accuses in v. 5: "You, you hypocrite, cast out the log from your own eye." Why such a harsh statement to his disciples, and why the

opening imperative: "Judge not?" All the Sermon seems
to require some judging. There is surely some irony in
the statement.   How can one avoid making preferences,
distinguishing   between   good   and   bad,   analyzing
situations?

        If the disciples will carefully work through
the paragraph they will discover its meaning. Although
the paragraph begins with the command to judge not, it
concludes with the admonition to remove the speck from
the brother's eye. To judge implies a standard which
is held up before or compared with the thing or person
being judged.   What then is the standard implied in
"judge not?" The standard immediately at hand is the
teaching Jesus has just given.   It has modified the
ancient   scripture.   It   is   spoken   in   terms   of
righteousness which includes worthy actions appropriate
to the disciples' right relation to God. Its standards
have created some degree of anxiety in the disciples.
The Sermon is a standard. If judging is the topic of
discussion, it can only imply that the Sermon is the
standard to be used in the judging process. Now that
is just the point that Jesus wishes to clarify. Judge
not!   "Do not use these teachings of mine as an
opportunity to judge your fellow disciple and decide
how well he has done what I've taught because it can be
applied to yourself as well."   There would be many
possible conclusions to which a disciple might come if
he used the Sermon to judge his fellow disciple. He is
a sinner. He has not measured up to Jesus' teaching.
He has failed here but succeeded there. He hasn't done
as well as I. None of this was intended by Jesus. The
disciples were not to use his teaching as a pretext to
self-righteousness.

        The intention of Jesus for the use of the
Sermon becomes apparent in the hyperbole proper,
beginning in verse 3.   The attention is immediately
focused on the potential judge, the subject of the
action.   This one must first attend to his own
condition, and the criteria by which he measures
himself will be Jesus' instruction.   Jesus' teaching
becomes a mirror for the disciple to remove the scandal
from   his   own   disposition   and   action.   The   Sermon
becomes an instrument for introspection and self-
evaluation.

        When the Sermon has been properly used by a
disciple inwardly then he is permitted "to take the
speck out of your brother's eye." In this concluding
line the tone is completely changed.   The paragraph

began almost harshly by prohibiting judgment. It
concludes by permitting healing. Now that the
"subject" disciple has properly applied the Sermon to
himself, he becomes an agent of healing and
rehabilitation rather than a self-righteous judge. The
Sermon has changed the "subject" first. Its proper use
is for introspection and self-evaluation.

The next brief statement almost seems out of
place, but on further consideration it addresses the
issue of how to use the Sermon.

> Do not give dogs what is holy; and do not throw
> your pearls before swine, lest they trample them
> underfoot and turn to attack you.

Mt. 7:6

This sentence is both humorous and hyperbolic
like the speck and the log. Dogs with holy objects and
swine with pearls is a laughing matter and an
exaggeration to think it could happen. The disciples
would recognize that as a proverb standing alone it
makes sense and could be applied in numerous
contexts. Here it is an extension of vv. 1-5 in that
again it teaches how the Sermon is to be used, or
rather how not to use it. The proverb teaches
discernment in handling precious matters. No one
places valuable materials at the disposal of those who
have no appreciation for them. Likewise, the disciples
have a precious possession in the Sermon. They must
use it with discernment. The isolated portions of the
Sermon without an understanding of its presuppositions
and manner of use would not be accepted or
understood. The disciples must recognize this.

> Ask and it will be given you; seek, and you
> will find; knock, and it will be opened to you.
> For everyone who asks receives, and he who seeks
> finds, and to him who knocks it will be opened. Or
> what man of you, if his son asks him for a loaf,
> will give him a stone? Or if he asks for a fish,
> will give him a serpent? If you then, who are
> evil, know how to give good gifts to your children,
> how much more will your Father who is in heaven
> give good things to those who ask him? So whatever
> you wish that men would do to you, do so to them;
> for this is the law and the prophets.

Mt. 7:7-12

In the third paragraph of this section the text turns away from hyperbolic humor and in a series of three rapidly phrased imperatives alerts the disciples to a different mood--"ask," "seek," "knock." The imperatives have lost the negative. They are written in the positive. The results of acting on the imperatives seem redundant. For example:

v. 7 Ask, and it will be given you.
v. 8 For everyone who asks receives.

v. 7 Seek, and you will find.
v. 8 He who seeks finds.

v. 7 Knock, and it will be opened to you,
v.   To him who knocks it will be opened.

This is a carry-over from Hebrew poetic parallelism and serves the function here of intensifying the paragraph and emphasizing its importance. Likewise the three imperatives, ask, seek, and knock, are not three steps in the process but are reiterating the urgency of the matter.

The disciples are held in suspense regarding the object or substance of the asking, seeking, knocking; and their attention is deflected from pursuing that until they are reminded of their own human goodness. They know how to respond to the requests of their children. Then they are told that "your Father who is in heaven" will answer their petition. This identifies the beginning imperative as prayer or petition to the heavenly Father, who will hear and respond.

Why has the matter of urgent prayer been re-introduced just now? The preceding context has instructed the disciples how to use, or not to use, the Sermon; but, so far, the real issue of how a disciple actualizes the ideals of the Sermon has not been clarified. This paragraph on prayer is the answer. The "it" in verses 7 and 8 is the "kingdom and his righteousness" which is asked for from God. On the one hand the prayer--asking, seeking, knocking--is a confession on the part of the disciple that he does not have the kingdom; at the same time it is his statement of sincere longing for what he does not have the natural means to attain. On the other hand the prayer recognizes that the "kingdom and his righteousness" is a gift from God. This is the clue to the disciples' implementing the demands of the Sermon--prayer!

The disciples have been prepared for this
paragraph by prior material in the Sermon. Three times
in chapter 6 Jesus said to the disciples "your Father
. . . will reward you" (6:4,6,18) and in that context
he has taught them to address God as "our Father;" and
once earlier they are asked to "pray for those who
persecute you" (5:44). The theme of prayer and its
importance is given a prominent place by Jesus in the
text of the Sermon. It emerges in every chapter at a
point where human ability to accomplish what is
required is in question. Can the disciples love their
enemies? Are they able to maintain the proper
motivation? Will they be able to actualize the
Sermon? The resolution to each question is given in a
reference to prayer. In the same contexts the rewards
of prayer are made known. The disciples will be sons
of the Father (5:45), they will receive rewards from
him (6:4,6,18), and they will receive what they ask
(7:8). It is not accidental that one of the words for
prayer is "seek," recalling "seek first his kingdom"
(6:33). The disciples now understand how to seek "his
kingdom."

Prayer then becomes the key for the disciples'
ability to actualize the Sermon. In addition to that
it brings some of the contrasting themes identified
through the Sermon into final focus. The
heavenly/earthly and the God/man themes are
finalized. God is in heaven, and the heavenly
dimension has made its demands on the earthly sphere
where man lives. If God and man, heaven and earth, are
to maintain a harmonious relation, it will come through
man's asking in prayer for the heavenly Father to grant
it. The heavenly/earthly and God/man themes have been
repeated constantly through the Sermon:

kingdom of heaven	(6 times)	5:3,10,19 (bis), 20; 7:21
heaven	(4 times)	5:12,34; 6:10,20
Father in heaven	(10 times)	5:16,45,48; 6:1,9,14,26, 32; 7:11,21
kingdom	(2 times)	6:10,33

All of this emphasis comes to rest in this paragraph
which is the last time "your Father in heaven" appears
in the Sermon.

The theme of the disciple's relation to his
fellowman (man/man) is brought to a conclusion here
with the recitation of the proverbial statement: "So

whatever you wish that men would do to you, do so to them." In concert with the disciples' ability to understand the clue to their actualizing the Sermon, they are taught that their relation to their fellowman will be resolved. The gift of the Sermon includes right relation with others.

While not explicit the other two contrasting themes are potential in this paragraph. The Sermon itself demands a correlation between inner thought, the heart, and the outward action. It also has noted the reflective nature of man and his actions. Those who ask, seek, and knock are "poor in spirit." They are "meek." They "hunger and thirst." They "mourn." Those who are able to do unto others are merciful, pure in heart, peacemakers, and willing to be persecuted. Thus the inner, reflective attitudes are brought into harmony with outward acts.

This paragraph ends with "for this is the law and prophets." The attentive disciple will recall the statement early in the Sermon: "I have come not to abolish but to fulfill the law and the prophets." Thus, when the disciples have been taught the true values of the kingdom and how to actualize them adequately, Jesus concludes in this text that the beginning intention of the Sermon has been accomplished.

Prayer, emphasized by asking, seeking, knocking, is the climax of the Sermon. It brings together all the themes and intentions introduced in the Sermon and assures the disciples of the heavenly Father's willingness to give them the gift of the kingdom. The disciples could imagine the teaching session was concluded with this paragraph, but not yet, for there are four more brief words from the teacher.

The next two paragraphs extend the concern for the necessity of proper discernment introduced in verse 6.

Enter by the narrow gate; for the gate is wide and the way is easy, that leads to destruction, and those who enter by it are many. For the gate is narrow and the way is hard, that leads to life, and those who find it are few.

Mt. 7:13f

88   Actualizing The Ideal

Jesus continues the pedagogical method of contrasts by
using the imagery of the narrow and wide gates. They
contrast the right and wrong ways of life. This
contrast has a long tradition in Hebrew religion.

> Behold, I set before you this day a blessing
> and a curse: the blessing, if you obey the
> commandments of the Lord your God, which I command
> you this day, and the curse, if you do not obey the
> commandments of the Lord your God, but turn aside
> from the way which I command you this day, to go
> after other gods which you have not known.

                                          Dt. 11:26-29

The Deuteronomy quotation makes the obedience to the
commandments the difference between the blessing and
the curse. There is no way of knowing if Jesus and his
disciples were consciously aware of the relation of his
teaching and this quotation, but the contrast of the
two ways was well known in religious circles, for the
Rabbis interpreted this Deuteronomy text as "two
ways."[1] Deuteronomy 30:15 and Jeremiah 21:8 contrast
the way of life and way of death. The Dead Sea
Scrolls, slightly earlier than Jesus, contrasts the
sons of light and the sons of darkness. So Jesus is
using a typical contrast in Hebrew religious circles.
The imagery continued in early Christian literature
outside the New Testament. The late first century work
entitled The Didache contrasts the way of life and the
way of death. As it elaborates the way of life it
paraphrases much of what is in Mt. 5.

Jesus' contrasts are the narrow gate that leads
to life and the wide gate that leads to destruction.
For Jesus the way of life is represented by his
Sermon. It is that which makes known "our Father" and
"his kingdom and his righteousness." Any other way is
disasterous. So Jesus in this text confronts the
disciples with the necessity of exercising their
discernment and making a choice in favor of the right
way. Even if the disciples have clearly understood
that the life of the Sermon is attained only as a gift
from the Father through their asking in prayer, they
must choose to ask for it. They must make the
conscious decision in favor of the kingdom
righteousness as articulated in the Sermon. God offers

---

[1]W. F. Albright and C. S. Mann, Matthew (New
York: Doubleday & Company, Inc., 1971), p. 184.

the gift; the disciples must choose to request it.[2]
They must discern that the Sermon is worthy to be
actualized in their lives and choose to ask God for
it. That is entering the narrow gate.

The disciples must not only choose in favor of
Jesus' teaching as the way that leads to life, they
must also discern the difference between right and
wrong religious prophets.

Beware of false prophets, who come to you in
sheep's clothing but inwardly are ravenous
wolves. You will know them by their fruits. Are
grapes gathered from thorns, or figs from
thistles? So, every sound tree bears good fruit,
but the bad tree bears evil fruit. A sound tree
cannot bear evil fruit, nor can a bad tree bear
good fruit. Every tree that does not bear good
fruit is cut down and thrown into the fire. Thus
you will know them by their fruits.

Mt. 7:15-20

This requires mental effort on the part of the
disciples. They must be familiar enough with the
instruction from Jesus that they can detect those who
are not true and sincere. The disciple must compare
the prophet's religious utterances which purport to
come from a pure heart with the prophet's overt actions
which are observed. It is the correlation between
these two that are important, for in the Sermon there
has been a continued concern for a sincere heart that
produces appropriate action. Jesus criticized those
who acted from an insincere heart for the praise of
men. The disciples must carefully discern the
difference between the true and false prophet.

This admonition is not contradictory to the
prohibition to judging in 7:1f. Here the object of
concern is with one who assumes the position of a
religious leader with an authoritative message from God
and who seeks to impress men so that they accept his
authenticity and follow him. The auditor or follower
must carefully discern the reliability of the prophet,
for he is placing his life in his hands. This is quite

---

[2]For this interpretation I am indebted to John
Wick Bowman, The Sermon from the Mount (Philadelphia:
Westminster Press, 1957), pp. 151-64.

different from the inclination of a disciple using
Jesus' teaching to put down a fellow disciple instead
of using the Sermon for self-analysis and brotherly rehabilitation.

The gravity of the matter is measured by the
harsh conclusion of Jesus that every tree, i.e.
prophet, that does not bear good fruit should be
removed. The problem of false prophets was as old as
the Hebrew religion itself as attested by Deuteronomy
13:1-3. Jesus wants his disciples to be ready to
practice good discretion when the occasion arises. In
fact they are involved in a test case at the very
moment of Jesus' teaching. Is he a false or a true
prophet? Does his action match his utterances? How do
they judge Jesus? The disciples were obliged to make a
choice to follow or not to follow, to be faithful or
not to be faithful. There were other teachers in
Israel at that time. Which one would the disciples
choose to follow? They must make a decision.

The importance of the disciples' decision is
the focus of the last two paragraphs of the Sermon.
There is a significant variant, however. There is a
grammatical change from the intimate second person
"you" to the generalized third person "everyone." This
movement from intimate to general brings the end of the
Sermon into symmetry with the opening of the Sermon
where it was observed that the introductory poem was in
the third person but gave way to the second person
(5:11) in an effort to bring the disciples into
closeness with the teacher. Now a sense of distance or
expansion is felt as the Sermon closes.

Not every one who says to me, "Lord, Lord,"
shall enter the kingdom of heaven, but he who does
the will of my Father who is in heaven. On that
day many will say to me, "Lord, Lord, did we not
prophesy in your name, and cast out demons in your
name, and do many mighty works in your name?" And
then will I declare to them, "I never knew you;
depart from me, you evil-doers."

Mt. 7:21-23

The contrast this time is between those who
only speak honorific titles of Jesus and those who
actually do the will of "my Father who is in heaven."
Jesus has used the first person "I" frequently in the
text of the Sermon as in the phrase "but I say to
you." In so doing he has claimed the authority of a

teacher and implied more as he contrasted his teaching
with the Hebrew scriptures. Now he claims himself and
his Father's will as the criteria for entering the
kingdom. "My Father's will" has been the subject of
the entire Sermon. It is the substance of God's will
for man. Thus, the disciples' response to Jesus and
his teaching is a response to God.

It is striking that the text uses an action
word in the phrase, "he who does." As the Sermon has
stressed throughout, the response to Jesus must be more
than an outward display. It must be outward actions
founded on an inner sincerity motivated from a desire
to please "our Father." As the paragraph continues,
Jesus remains the focal point, and in the day of
judgment he will be the one to whom some plead their
case, and he will decide their destiny. Jesus pictures
himself in the role of a judge who takes into account
the inner motivation rather than only observing some
outer display of unusual religious acts.

The disciples would be impressed by the demand
being made in this paragraph. They are reminded again
that to actualize the ideals of the Sermon they must
have the proper inner disposition. It is not enough to
simply "do." Nor is it enough to be "pure of heart."
Instead there must be righteous conduct, pleasing to
God, emanating from a sincere inner disposition.

This paragraph is designed to maintain the
proper relation between Jesus and his disciples. He
has drawn close to them by using the intimate "I-you"
grammatical construction and has frequently spoken of
"your Father in heaven" and even taught them to say
"our Father." Now he drops the "I-you" phrase and
moves to the less personal "everyone." When he
mentions God, the phrase is "my Father," reminding the
disciples that it is he and only he who brings
knowledge of God to man. Only Jesus in the Sermon, or
in the Gospels anywhere, uses the singular pronoun "my"
with Father. Jesus here declares his intimate special
relation with God. Jesus' use of "my Father" at this
point is the only time that he refers to God by this
manner in the Sermon, and it is the last time "Father"
appears in the Sermon. This emphasizes Jesus' special
relation to God. In addition to this Jesus pictures
himself in the role of judge. The disciples are
herewith instructed that Jesus' teaching is founded on
his claim to a unique relation with God and his
position as final judge.

The final paragraph of the Sermon is in the form of a parable.

> Every one then who hears these words of mine
> and does them will be like a wise man who built his
> house upon the rock; and the rain fell, and the
> floods came, and the winds blew and beat upon that
> house, but it did not fall, because it had been
> founded on the rock. And every one who hears these
> words of mine and does not do them will be like a
> foolish man who built his house upon the sand; and
> the rain fell, and the floods came, and the winds
> blew and beat against that house, and it fell; and
> great was the fall of it.

Mt. 7:24-27

The simple story has an obvious conclusion: How wise and sensible to build a house on a solid foundation; how unwise and ridiculous to build a house on shifting sand with no sure footing. The application is made by Jesus to "these words of mine." They are the criteria of judgment. When this paragraph is compared with the previous one, "these words of mine" equal "the will of my father." Doing Jesus' words pleases the Father in heaven. If the disciples wondered what was the content of "hunger and thirst for righteousness," or "thy will be done on earth," or "seek first his kingdom and his righteousness," they now understand. It is doing the words of Jesus just now conveyed to them. By actualizing Jesus' teaching they are participating in the kingdom and its righteousness. They are doing the will of the heavenly Father.

Here as in the previous paragraph the action word "does" is used. The disciple must not only hear he must also activate what he has heard. Jesus has instructed his disciples carefully; they have heard; now they must choose to act upon their instruction. The final paragraph climaxes this section with a challenge to decide in favor of the Sermon and act upon it.

The Reader: The Instructed

The final section of the Sermon opens with a jolting: "Do not judge;" but before the section ends the reader may feel some inconsistency since the disciples are taught to exercise discernment and Jesus himself judges. Paragraphs must not be set in opposiion to each other but rather should be seen as they develop the theme of the section. The reader who does this will have less difficulty with the apparent inconsistencies.

1. As the reader proceeds through this section he is well aware of the emphasis on the inner nature of the Sermon's instructions to the disciples. It must be used not as an instrument to judge their fellow disciples but rather to analyze their own disposition.

2. Their inner disposition must give expression to conduct pleasing to the Father in heaven. Thus the reflective/action contrasting themes are emphasized.

3. The reader is aware that the disciples are urged to make a decision in favor of the Sermon, its teacher, and the will of God. This is the righteousness taught throughout the Sermon.

4. The reader, like the disciples, cannot miss Jesus' emphasis on prayer. Only as the disciples recognize their dependency upon God through it, will they be able to please him.

5. Out of this context comes the recognition of the complementary nature of the ability to be an ideal disciple as a gift from God and the necessity of the disciple to choose in favor of it. This is how the God/man theme and the heavenly/earthly theme is resolved.

6. Out of the instruction on prayer, the reader learns how it is possible for the disciples to cope with the overwhelming demands of the Sermon.

7. The reader become aware that the responsibility for becoming involved in the kingdom and its righteousness rests with the disciples' willingness to choose.

CHAPTER VIII

MODERN DISCIPLES AND THE SERMON

And when Jesus finished these sayings, the crowds were astonished at his teaching, for he taught them as one who had authority, and not as their scribes. When he came down from the mountain, great crowds followed him.

Mt. 7:28-8:1

Although the instruction ends with 7:27, the Sermon has not been officially closed until the notation in the text, "When Jesus finished these sayings." The text further notes that the "crowds" were astonished. This may at first perplex the reader, but the reader must look again at the beginning and end of the teaching and ask why the text is so structured.

As the text in Chapter 4 moved toward the Sermon, it recorded that great crowds were following Jesus. Then Jesus withdrew, his disciples came, and he taught them, the disciples (5:1f.). Then the text opens with a poem in a very general tone and moves after eight verses to the personal, somewhat intimate, "you" directed to the disciples. This point of view is maintained until the last two paragraphs, only slightly longer than the opening poem, where the intimate "you" gives way to the generalized "everyone." The crowds come back into the narrative in 7:28f. and are further enlarged in 8:1. The sensitive reader detects a bit of artistry here. The text takes the form of an intimate teaching situation between Jesus and his disciples bracketed at beginning and end by the crowds. The reader is aware of this. The reader is an outsider, an observer. The text is aware of the reader's posture and makes an effort to draw the reader into the intimate session. So the text sets the stage for intimacy by reducing the crowds to only the disciples and then draws the reader into this intimacy by the use of the second person "you." At the end of the teaching the text must return the reader to his position outside the inner group and place him back in the crowd; the crowd at the end cannot be the crowd at the beginning because they have not heard the instructions. So a link is missing. While the ending of the teaching moves from intimate "you" to the generalized "everyone," the reverse of the beginning, the mention of the disciples is omitted and only the crowds respond. Literally, the crowds are the same from whom Jesus and his disciples withdrew in the beginning, but in the world of the text the crowds are the readers who have been drawn into the text. This is the text's way of engaging the reader and giving him the feeling that he is overhearing Jesus' instructions to his disciples. So the modern reader seriously reading the Sermon and its context, frequently asks himself the question "What is this saying to me?" The previous pages of this book have been written with the intention of helping to answer that question, i.e. how does one apply the Sermon today?

A Sermon Summary

A brief summary of the Sermon at this point will be helpful. The Sermon began with a description of the ideal disciple. He is poor in spirit, meek, longs for righteousness, merciful, pure in heart, a peacemaker, willing to be persecuted for righteousness. This ideal person is one who has had a deep and abiding experience of his own inadequacy, which has led him to an inner desire to have the right relation with God and his fellowman. He has had a religious experience. He wishes to be righteous and practice righteousness before God (5:3-16).

Jesus turns next in the Sermon to describe those things which constitute righteous conduct pleasing to God. Then he elaborates five paragraphs which have been identified as values: human existence, sexuality, integrity, self-respect, and love. These are the values on which the conduct of the disciples should be based. Jesus even gave illustrations of how to apply these values (5:17-48).

The disciples, as he seeks to implement the values pleasing to God, must be motivated properly (6:1-18). He can do this only as he is totally committed to the proper ultimate value--God (6:19-34).

Then the final section instructs the disciples to use the Sermon for self-analysis and impresses upon them the necessity of a decision in favor of Jesus and his instruction (7:1-27). The reader must also remember that the Gospel of Matthew closes with a command by Jesus to his first disciples that they must instruct new disciples all that he has taught them. This includes the Sermon on the Mount.

This brief summary brings out three steps in the development of the Sermon: (1) The values to be implemented, (2) what motivates one to implement the values, and (3) one must deliberately choose to be committed to the kingdom of righteousness.

Decision and Commitment

The first step in applying the Sermon is to recognize that the Sermon is given to those who are willing to decide in favor of and commit themselves to Jesus as the one who brings the true knowledge of "our Father" and what he wills for his children.[1] Loyalty to Jesus is required at the beginning of the Sermon when the disciples are told that they must be willing to be "persecuted on my account" (5:11); toward the end of the Sermon Jesus makes himself the center of loyalty and the ultimate judge (7:21ff); and in the last paragraph he sets as the criteria for that judgment the hearing and doing of "these words of mine." Jesus so intertwines himself with the Sermon that to accept one is to accept the other and to reject one is to reject the other.

This loyalty required by Jesus encompasses the right relation to God. Men are to long for and seek his kingdom (5:6; 6:34); they are willing to be persecuted for God's righteousness (5:10); they are to strive to be like God (5:48); they desire to be rewarded by God (6:1f.); and they choose to do his will (7:21). To be committed to Jesus is to be committed to God, and one is not possible without the other.

The authority of Jesus' teaching is recognized by those listening to him (7:28). It is also recognized throughout the Gospel and culminates in his post-resurrection appearance in Galilee where he declares: "All authority in heaven and on earth has been given to me" (28:18).[2]

---

[1]Although this is the third step in the development of the Sermon it seems the most logical beginning point in applying the Sermon.

[2]Cf. the author's article, "Matthew xxvii 16-20 and the Design of the First Gospel," Journal for the Study of the New Testament, X (January, 1981), 2-18.

The urgency for decision and commitment is vividly set forth in the last half of Matthew 7 in the choices between the two gates, the true and false prophets, those who say "Lord, Lord," and the two houses.

The modern disciple must not lose sight of this as he reads and rereads the Sermon. The Sermon itself has the potential to evoke a decision and commitment from the reader. Its lofty ethical standards challenge the sense of good and spiritual in a person. Its intimate tone from Jesus and the assurance that God "our Father in heaven" cares for us and knows our needs bring comfort to those who feel alienated from the world around them. The concluding stories that require a decision may so involve the reader that he will decide that the Sermon's message is appropriate and meaningful for him. The Sermon itself may be an instrument to make disciples.

On the other hand a disciple may already be committed when he comes to the Sermon. From whatever position one reads the Sermon the opening verses describe a religious experience. It has already been experienced by the disciple or something akin to it will be his experience. A review of the first four beatitudes will make the point clear.

"Blessed are the poor in spirit" was interpreted to refer to those who were without a sense of spiritual worth. They feel alienated and estranged from God and they recognize their need for him.

"Blessed are those who mourn" refers to those who deeply regret their alienation from God. It is a matter of deep grief and concern to them.

"Blessed are the meek" identified those who were willing to trust in God.

"Blessed are those who hunger and thirst for righteousness." They long for God's salvation.

These four beatitudes when taken together speak of man's inner spiritual concern as he seeks to be reconciled with God. A person coming from such an experience, or being provoked to such an experience, is ready to commit himself in loyalty and devotion to the demand of Jesus in the Sermon. He recognizes his spiritual need and he trusts God to satisfy it.

The teaching of the Sermon is based on the assumption that those who seek to implement it are sincerely devoted to Jesus and his representation of God. Thus the immediate implementation of the Sermon has its limitations. Not all people are ready to accept it as just described. Because of this the committed disciple must practice discernment in the way he uses the Sermon to apply to others. He will not, nor cannot, impose the ideals of the Sermon on those who do not accept Jesus' authority. It must be recalled that the basic purpose of the instruction in the Sermon was for self-reflection on the part of the disciple.

At the same time, a modern disciple may observe times and places in our world when it seems as if some aspect of the Sermon is held dear by those who do not recognize the total authority of Jesus. Since much of Jesus' instructions deals with basic human problems, it is not surprising that some serious thinkers have arrived at moral conclusions akin to Jesus! Christian ethics and ideals have in many ways filtered into Western society over the last two millenia and influenced the way people think.

Even though he might find expressions of concern in modern society similar to those in the Sermon, the modern disciple will be aware of a deeper motivation growing out of his spiritual experience with God in Jesus.

The Motivation

The decision and commitment of the modern disciple is a part of his inner spiritual experience. In that experience he will also be aware of the blessing of reconciliation with God. The burdening feeling of estrangement is lifted. He has the sense of the presence of God in his life. It is the feeling of the nearness of God that becomes the primary motivation to actualize the ideals of the Sermon in the life of the disciple.

"Our Father" in the model prayer expresses this concept more profoundly than any other section of the Sermon. This matter has been discussed before, but it is important enough to warrant further amplification. In all of the places where Jesus addresses God, he uses the term "Father" except in the cry from the cross, "My God, my God," which Jesus quoted from the opening line of Psalm 22:1. Yet the Greek forms of the word for "Father" are not all the same, sometimes nominative, sometimes vocative. This is explained as a variation in translating the original Aramaic speech of Jesus into Greek. The Gospel of Mark provides the clue in Jesus' prayer in 14:36 where the author retains the original Aramaic word for "Father," Abba, and then repeats the Greek word "Father." Mark's effort is to convey the specific connotation which Jesus gave to his address for God. The Greek address "Father" does not carry with it the same significance as the word Abba. Abba is the intimate, family name of endearment for "Father." It is thought to be one of the earliest words an Aramaic-speaking child would learn to say. Never was it used in formal prayers nor as an address to God until Jesus' innovation. The word Abba stands behind the English and Greek texts in those places where Jesus addresses God as "Father." He chose the intimate, affectionate term for God and taught his disciples to use it also.[3]

Not only did his immediate disciples use the term, they also taught second and third generation disciples to use this intimate address for God. Twice in Paul's writing he refers to the fact the believers can address God as "Abba! Father!" (Rom. 8:15; Gal. 4:6). These texts assume that his readers already knew the term. In both references in Paul, the phrase is used to emphasize and confirm that the believers have a relationship with God so close and unique that it must be described by the Father-son/child relation. This is not an innovative concept by the apostle, rather he has learned this from the very teaching of Jesus. His use helps the modern disciple understand how important this idea coming from Jesus was to the early believers.

The model prayer, opening with "our Father," was given by Jesus to his disciples only. The Sermon, as emphasized before, was addressed to those who were loyal to Jesus and his cause. The references in Paul's writing are given for believers only. The Didache, a late first century Christian writing, admonishes the new converts, after they have been baptized, to recite the prayer three times a day (8:3). As late as the

---

[3]The discussion of Abba is based on Joachim Jeremias, The Prayer's of Jesus (London: SCM Press, 1967); and The Lord's Prayer (Philadelphia: Fortress Press, 1964). The later title is readily available for most readers.

fourth century the prayer was recited in that part of
the worship service in which only believers were
present. This attests the "awesome reverence" with
which the early Christians used the model prayer. It
was not for them property of the general public but
rather an intimate moment of addressing the holy God
with the very words Jesus had taught.

For the disciple, both ancient and modern, to
address God as "our Father" is to recognize a close,
loving, intimate relationship between him and the holy
other God. It is to recognize that in the teaching and
example of Jesus the remote, hidden One has come
near. This closeness has been described by early
Christian writers and Jesus himself as the Father-
son/child relationship. The blessing of a disciple in
the beatitudes is "they shall see God," and "they shall
be called sons of God;" and in 5:45 Jesus encourages
the disciples to action so that they may be "sons of
your Father . . ." It is the obvious intention of
Jesus to include this closeness in the term "our
Father."

This term will also include the idea of
dependency which was earlier introduced in the
beatitudes "Blessed are the meek." It is reiterated in
other settings in the teachings of Jesus when he says,
"Unless you turn and become like children" (Mt.
18:3). In this text Jesus is cautioning his disciples
to remain humble which requires a continual
acknowledgement of their dependency upon a merciful
heavenly Father. The modern disciple must not
interpret "meekness," "dependency," or "humility" as a
description of the unwholesome dependency that one
human being can develop on another. Rather dependency
in the sense it is used here is a reference to the
reverent attitude of the believer toward God who has
graciously given of himself through Jesus Christ and
whom the disciple knows and loves because of this
gift. A disciple's new style of existence is dependent
on God.

The modern disciple, following this line of
thought, begins to be aware of the indescribable
blessing that Jesus has brought to him with the ability
to pray "our Father." Not only is he a child of God on
whom he can recognize his dependency, but he can also
be assured that the heavenly Father knows his need.
The model prayer is introduced with "Your Father knows
what you need before you ask him" (6:8). Later in the
same chapter, the disciple is assured that the heavenly

Father is sensitive to the needs of his children and
will care for them more abundantly than the things of
nature: "Your heavenly Father knows that you need them
all" (6:32). In the final prayer of the Sermon, Jesus
again reassures the disciple of the Father's
willingness to give the appropriate blessings to his
children (7:11).

To say "our Father" with the implied relation
of Father-son/child is to recognize that God is a
model. A cliche found in ancient literature is the
phrase "son of _____" with a word indicating the
quality or characteristic attributed to the person
being described. Jesus calls James and John "sons of
thunder" (Mk. 3:17). One could be called a son of joy,
peace, or any other suitable quality. The thinking of
oneself as "son of God" does indeed suggest that he in
some way is like God. This is in keeping with Jesus'
command: "You, therefore, must be perfect, as your
heavenly Father is perfect" (5:38).

All of this gives the modern disciple a
strange, awesome, reverent feeling that the heavenly
Father is a present reality in his human life. All
that has been said on this point can be summarized in
the two words--"our Father." To utter this phrase is a
prayer, a prayer that recognizes all of the
implications that fill this term--all the blessings,
reassurances, forgiveness, reconciliation, sense of
nearness of the heavenly Father--all that Jesus taught
both in his Sermon and elsewhere. To speak these words
audibly or in the heart is an expression of the
disciple's commitment and devotion to Jesus and the
heavenly Father.

The corporate nature of the phrase is present
in the plural "our." The heavenly Father does not
belong to "me" but to the whole body of disciples. So
the modern disciple is aware of the great host of
fellow believers who share the same commitment that he
does as he utters this prayer. Is a disciple not
permitted to make his prayer more intimate than
"our?" Can he never say "My?" So long as he does not
think of God as his sole possession, yes he can address
him as "my heavenly Father." Jesus in the context of
the model prayer spoke of "your (singular) heavenly
Father" five times (6:4, 6 bis, 18 bis); and in the
references in Paul's writing the believers have learned
to address God as Abba on a one-to-one basis. "Our" or
"my" is not emphasizing the singularity or plurality of
the disciples' praying but rather the close loving

intimate nature of the relationship. So a modern disciple can address God as "Abba, my Father" with all the connotation described above.

This new relationship which permits the disciple to say "our Father" is the motivation to actualize the will of God which is expressed in the words of Jesus in the Sermon. Motivation--what causes a person to act--in the Sermon on the Mount is the new relationship that the disciple has with "our Father." Out of this relationship comes the desire and intention to do "the will of my Father who is in heaven" and "these words of mine."

Implementing the Values

The modern disciple who has decided and committed himself to the heavenly Father so that he can utter "our Father" must seek to implement the values taught by Jesus in the Sermon. There are five of these in Matthew 5 and discussed in this work in chapter 3. One of the major problems in implementing these values is the fact that not all men accept them in the same way that a committed believer does. While many may have respect for the umbrella value there will be sincere differences in the way to apply them. Likewise the modern disciple will not find unanimity among believers on how to implement the values. The disciple should not be discouraged by this, rather he should recall that the Sermon teaches that he is "light" and "salt" to the world around him, and by demonstrating suitable values he will bring something of Jesus' teaching into each human situation.

The value of human existence as discussed by Jesus certainly teaches the modern disciple to have absolute respect for the life of each human being. It is the ideal that the disciple maintain gracious and friendly relations with every human being in his orbit of life. These can be far reaching and complicated: members of the same family, associates in business, fellow workers, store clerks, sub-way token sellers, taxi drivers, etc. Must the modern disciples stop to relate to all of these people? Obviously not! He does, however, have an occasion to treat kindly or mistreat many people along the way. How then is this value applicable? The disciple should never have degrading thoughts or actions toward any of the countless number of people he meets from day to day. He should recall that each person whom he meets was created by God and is potentially one who can find the same reconciled relation that he enjoys, uttering "our Father."

There is no way to deduce a long system of minute rules to cover every eventuality of life, but experience has certainly given some examples. It is degrading to another human being to utter idle gossip about him. It is degrading to another human being to take from him possessions that are meaningful to him. It is degrading to impose physical harm on a person. A sincere disciple will avoid inner thoughts that degrade his fellowman lest he act unworthily toward him. The disciple must remember that this value, like the others, emphasized the inner attitude of the disciple toward his fellowman. From the proper inner disposition comes worthy deeds.

When Jesus taught this value in Mt. 5:21-26 he used illustrations at the interpersonal level where a disciple had some degree of control over the situation and his response to it. That is to say, Jesus explained the matter at the level of the disciple's comprehension and ability to handle the matter. This is important to recognize. The individual lives every day relating to others, often the same set of contacts reoccur over a span of time. In his everyday experiences with others he must constantly be aware of the value of human life and seek to implement it daily. In so doing he is being "light" and "salt" to his own world however limited. Out of this limited experience will come understanding for the more complex issues of life.

Jesus' discussion of the law, "Thou shall not kill,"--the value of human existence--usually brings out the question of war, incarceration, capital punishment, police restraint, self-defense, and related subjects. The questions may be asked, "How does Jesus' teaching apply?" Jesus' teaching sets an ideal standard for the disciple's attitude toward his fellowman. He makes no exceptions. How then can a modern disciple apply Jesus' teaching to global situations that seem to contradict the ideal? First, he must recognize that he lives in an imperfect world in which imperfect people are applying imperfect solutions to problems created by other imperfect men. Some involved in this process may be sincere disciples. Second, a sincere disciple may be forced to choose between alternatives, none of which are ideal. Shall a prisoner be retained in confinement in an undesirable environment or shall he be released to an ineffective parole system? Third, even in an imperfect situation a disciple has the possibility of lobbying for the best possible solution in keeping with the ideals he holds. Thus, some disciples with good conscience participate in just wars, deterrent actions, and police restraint with the belief that such action is to be preferred over disorder and chaos, and always longing for the accomplishment of Jesus' ideal. Other equally sincere disciples will conclude that the only response to war is strict pacifism, convinced that by their testimony they will inspire others to join them, giving allegiance to the ideal of Jesus.

Jesus' ideal is clear. The disciple's attitude toward his fellowman must be one of goodwill and reconciliation, no abuse or degradation. Even, if there are differences of opinion on some larger issues, each disciple has the opportunity to actualize this ideal in his daily encounter, thus being "salt" and "light" to his world, however small. If each disciple achieved this in his own world, how great the light would be!

The reflective, sincere, disciple will often feel a tension between the ideals he identifies in the teaching of Jesus and life as he finds it in his world. Since the world of men has not accepted the ideal of Jesus, this tension is unavoidable. The tug between what one holds as ideal and what is can produce a sense of failure and even guilt on the part of the disciple. When this happens there is a tendency to modify the ideal so it will be in keeping with human attainment. The text of the Sermon does not allow that. It is better for the disciple to recognize his own failure as well as that of others and return to his primary source of motivation and utter "our Father" with all of its implications. He can then begin afresh the life of a sincere disciple. This is recognizing again that he is "poor in spirit" and can only accomplish the will of the heavenly Father as he experiences forgiveness and reconciliation. This blessing of forgiveness and realignment is in keeping with the Sermon and more satisfying to the disciple than modifying the ideal to fit the affairs of men.

The value of sexuality as discussed in the text of the Sermon recognized the need for a proper relation between man and woman both within and outside the marriage vow. The text is written from a man's point of view since the society of the first century was so oriented. In spite of this, when compared with teachers contemporary with him, Jesus' teaching is a major step forward in recognizing the unfavorable position society had imposed upon women.

The modern disciple will observe that Jesus spoke specifically about divorce; and, because it has become an accepted practice in modern times, one is inclined to begin there. This should not be done, but rather recall that the basic point is a comment on the lustful look of a man toward a woman. This puts the beginning discussion in the area of attitudes. The appeal is simple and can be broadened for the modern disciple: "One should not make lust the basis of relating to the opposite sex." The importance of this admonition is given in the hyperbole that follows (5:29f.).

All that has been said about the value of human existence could be repeated here; for, when a sincere disciple relates to someone of the opposite sex, that someone is a fellow human being and deserves all of the respect and goodwill noted above. That one is, or potentially, one who can say "our Father;" he/she is one whom God has created either male or female; therefore, there is more involved in the relation of man and woman than simply "lust." At whatever stage of life the modern disciple is--youth, young adult, middle years, or older, married, or single--his/her attitude toward the opposite sex must be measured by the ideal of the Sermon.

If the ideal value of human existence and respect for the opposite sex has been genuinely internalized, the specific instruction on divorce will be less difficult. The text is quite clear that by divorcing the husband puts the wife in a sinful state. This is not appropriate. Literally, the text does not say: "Thou shalt not divorce." It simply says, if you do, here is what happens. Of course, the onus of being labeled an adulterer was more than one could bear in the society of Jesus' day.

The modern disciple must remember that the ideal Jesus is describing is not for all of society but for those have learned to utter "our Father." If the disciple has internalized the values of human existence, and if he has proper respect for the opposite sex, and if he values an integrated life, and if he has the proper understanding of self-respect, what earthly eventuality would require a divorce? If

both partners are committed to the values of Jesus and
have learned to say "our Father," what human
difficulties cannot be overcome? It was the faith of
the early Christians that their domestic lifestyle
witnessed to the reality of their new life in
Christ.[4] The modern disciple has that possibility
also.

     In his teaching on divorce Jesus is giving the
ideal of what marriage should be as intended from
creation. As disciples live under the will of God and
measure up to the total words of Jesus, they will find
fulfillment in an indissoluble oneness in their
marriage and will rejoice that they have been able to
be "light" and "salt" for the world about them.[5]

     But what of those who chose to end their
marriage in divorce, even more who strive to be sincere
disciples? Modern disciples should remember that there
are two parts to Jesus' teaching. On the one hand he
makes absolute demands and sets high ideals. On the
other hand he teaches the compassionate love of the
heavenly Father who forgives. Whenever any disciple
falls short of any ideal in Jesus' teaching, he can
return to that moment when he first learned to utter
"our Father," and there find forgiveness,
reconciliation, and renewed motivation to strive for
the life to which he is committed. This will apply to
divorce also. It is not necessary for the divorced
person, friends, or clerics to devise casuistic schemes
to legitimatize the process. The disciple needs only
to find restoration and peace with "our Father."

     The value of integrity when discussed in
Chapter IV was based on a text that dealt with
truthfulness. There it was reasoned that a lifestyle
based on a distortion of truth and reality were
symptons of a personality that lacked integration and
wholeness. While the value of always telling the truth
and being sincerely honest seems simple enough, they
are basic to the character of the sincere disciple. In
simple matters, he makes only promises which he can

_____

     [4]I interpret the following references as
evidence for this point: Eph. 5:21-6:9; Col. 3:18-4:6;
and I Pet. 2:18-3:7.

     [5]Myrna and Robert Kysar, The Asundered
(Atlanta: John Knox Press, 1978), pp. 53ff.

keep, he avoids exaggeration, he has no need of self-
aggrandizement. The modern disciple has no need of
being less than truthful and honest. He knows that he
is a child of God. He has developed a worthy self-
image and feels secure in his relation to others. He
has nothing to hide because he has goodwill and respect
for his fellowman.

This value spills over into the other values.
In fact, one should never assume that the values are
isolated from one another. The value of integrity
supports the value of human existence and the value of
sexuality. At the same time those values enhance the
disciple's integrity.

The value of self-respect is important for the
modern disciple. Each generation defines what brings a
sense of self-esteem, and all human beings seek to
attain some degree of satisfaction in his pursuit for a
worthy self-image. This grows out of his family
background as well as his larger environment. The
sincere disciple must realize that his commitment to
Jesus' ideals brings with it a new self-
understanding. He is now a child of God who can
address him as "our Father." Therefore, he does not
have to depend on traditional standards of self-
respect. Instead he feels a sense of satisfaction as
he lives within the will of God, which includes the
desire to establish peace in difficult situations and
bring rehabilitation in broken relations. He had
rather give up his rights if it means letting his light
shine as a child of God.

Of course, the question can be asked how far
must the disciple go in giving up his rights or giving
in to those who make demands upon him? It is more
politeness to give up a seat in a public hall if it is
claimed by you and someone else, or to give over a
place in traffic to another motorist; but there are
more difficult situations. Does one give up his
candidacy to public office because a fellow disciple is
a candidate for the same office? Does a sincere
disciple really give to everyone who asks a donation?
Does he never resist when government imposes an unfair
burden: taxes, draft, and other requirements?

Again, the interpersonal matters are somewhat
simple to handle. When a disciple is confronted with a
demand from a fellow human being, the primary concern
should be peacemaking and goodwill. It is possible to
say "no" and retain goodwill. The disciple who

practices this value at the individual level will gain
insight as he moves into the more complex social and
civil demands. As he deals with situations in which he
alone is concerned for kingdom values, it will be more
difficult and he may not always find the best solution;
however, his goal will always be to bring peace and
reconciliation into the affairs of men.

     The value of love has been identified as the
summary value. To speak of love alone is not enough.
Unless love is given form and substance it has little
significance and is in danger of being distorted. The
modern disciple will note from the text that love is
patterned after God who is the source of love. The
modern disciple who has learned to utter "our Father"
understands better the meaning of love than before he
was reconciled to God. He has experienced divine love
which motivates him to express love. God's love does
not discriminate between good and bad, friends and
enemies. So the disciple as he relates to others will
not be selective either. All of the values and the
resultant conduct is extended by the disciples to every
person he meets. He does not adjust his personality
and actions to the beautiful, sophisticated, or well-
to-do. He is the same to all men. His sense of self-
respect, worth of human existence, his integrity, and
respect for the opposite sex guides his attitudes and
acts for every person. This is the expression of
love. Love is fulfilling the values articulated by
Jesus.

EPILOGUE

The modern disciple will read and reread the Sermon on the Mount. Each time he will discover new insights in the will of God in these words of Jesus. From them he will discover the values that design his life and direct his conduct. From its pages he will learn to say "our Father." Of all the words in the Sermon these two summarize all that it means to be a committed disciple. Out of a new sense of self-identity, assurance of forgiveness, joy of reconciliation, that comes from these two words a disciple is able to actualize the teachings of Jesus in the Sermon. And if--if we should fail or fall short at some point in our earthly pilgrimage, God's gracious love and forgiveness will bring us to utter again "our Father."

BIBLIOGRAPHY

Betz, Hans Dieter. Essays on the Sermon on the Mount. Philadelphia: Fortress Press, 1984.

Bonhoeffer, Dietrich. The Cost of Discipleship. Translated by R. H. Fuller. New York: The MacMillan Company, 1963.

Bowman, John Wick. The Gospel from the Mount. Philadelphia: The Westminster Press, 1957.

Davies, W. D. The Setting of the Sermon on the Mount. Cambridge: at the University Press, 1966.

Dibelius, Martin. The Sermon on the Mount. New York: Charles Scribner's Sons, 1940.

Friedlander, Gerald. The Jewish Sources of the Sermon on the Mount. New York: Ktav Publishing House, 1969.

Guelich, Robert A. The Sermon on the Mount. Waco: Word Books Publisher, 1982.

Jeremias, Joachim. The Sermon on the Mount. Translated by Norman Perrin. Philadelphia: Fortress Press, 1963.

Kissinger, Warren S. The Sermon on the Mount: A History of Interpretation and Bibliography. Metuchen, N.J.: Scarecrow Press, 1975.

McArthur, Harvey K. Understanding the Sermon on the Mount. New York: Harper and Row, 1960.

Thielicke, Helmut. Life Can Begin Again. Translated by John W. Doberstein. Philadelphia: Fortress Press, 1963.

Thompson, Ernest Trice. The Sermon on the Mount; And Its Meaning for Today. Richmond: John Knox Press, 1953.

Thurneysen, Eduard. Sermon on the Mount. Translated by William Childs Robinson. Richmond: John Knox Press, 1964.

Windisch, Hans. The Meaning of the Sermon on the Mount. Translated by S. MacLean Gilmour. Philadelphia: The Westminster Press, 1951.